CONFESSIONS OF A SELF-CARE JUNKIE

A Woman's Journey to Loving Herself and Living Free

CHRISTY PRIMMER

BALBOA.PRESS

A DIVISION OF HAY HOUSE

Balboa Press books may be ordered through booksellers or by contacting:

Balboa Press
A Division of Hay House
1663 Liberty Drive
Bloomington, IN 47403
www.balboapress.com
844-682-1282

Because of the dynamic nature of the Internet, any web addresses or links contained in this book may have changed since publication and may no longer be valid. The views expressed in this work are solely those of the author and do not necessarily reflect the views of the publisher, and the publisher hereby disclaims any responsibility for them.

The author of this book does not dispense medical advice or prescribe the use of any technique as a form of treatment for physical, emotional, or medical problems without the advice of a physician, either directly or indirectly. The intent of the author is only to offer information of a general nature to help you in your quest for emotional and spiritual well-being. In the event you use any of the information in this book for yourself, which is your constitutional right, the author and the publisher assume no responsibility for your actions.

Print information available on the last page.

ISBN: 978-1-9822-6011-8 (sc)
ISBN: 978-1-9822-6013-2 (hc)
ISBN: 978-1-9822-6012-5 (e)

Library of Congress Control Number: 2020924095

Balboa Press rev. date: 01/05/2021

To women searching outside of themselves for approval and acceptance. May you learn more about who you are and ask with confidence for what you need without apologizing. It's time for you to spread your wings and fly free.

CONTENTS

SPIRITUAL SELF-CARE

MENTAL WELLNESS SELF-CARE

PHYSICAL WELL-BEING SELF-CARE

SEXUAL HEALTH + BLISS SELF-CARE

EMOTIONAL STABILITY SELF-CARE

FINANCIAL HEALTH SELF-CARE

INTRODUCTION

My name is Christy, and I have a *confession* to make.

I used to hide who I was for fear of not fitting in or being abandoned. I spent many years downplaying my worth in all relationships. I apologized for being *too* loud, *too* big, *too* bold, and *too* different. It was exhausting. I no longer apologize for being me, to anyone. I no longer engage in relationships, conversations, or any other thing that asks me to.

I knew all along that I was different. I'll dive into examples of why throughout this book. I now know that being different has always been my ticket to freedom. I had big dreams as a young girl. Dreams that were unrealistic for a girl like me. Somehow, I knew. I knew I was going to help change the world. I spent a lot of time digging ditches that I'd eventually have to climb out of as I sifted and sorted through challenges and choices on my journey to becoming the woman I am today. I can't say I am 100 percent satisfied, because I am always wanting to improve myself, be better, and do more, no matter how great my life is (*and it is really great!*); however, I can say I love myself inside out. I can say I live free—free of others opinions and expectations, for the most part. I wrote this book because I want that kind of real, liberating freedom for you too. I have a confession to make about who I am. I am a self-love and self-care junkie. I cannot get enough, ever. Loving myself inside out has completely transformed my life. I want that same kind of inner transformation for you.

I am over-the-moon addicted to being unapologetically more me every day in all things. It's like once I broke out of the container society tried to squish me into, things became easier, and my life got better. The positive thoughts and feelings I started having about myself became extremely addictive. I stopped hurting myself with negative addictions and started to thrive in a way I had never imagined. I want that for you too.

I wrote this book to tell you that some addictions do not require treatment or therapy. Some addictions (think prayer, bath bombs, speaking your truth, dark chocolate, creating boundaries, and aqua fit) are the remedy. You cannot experience next-level joy using old thoughts and behavior. Investing in yourself leads to so many endless possibilities, but you've got to figure out how exactly you need to take care of yourself. No one can tell you what self-care practices or routines you need to do. There is no one-size-fits-all approach to healing. What I will tell you is that once you start filling up your cup, you will never be thirsty again. Now, let's address something right off the hop. According to *Merriam-Webster*, the word *addiction* means 1: the quality or state of being addicted // addicted to reading is the given example. The word *addicted* is all about having to do something repeatedly. Taking care of yourself will become your healthiest addiction, if you allow it to. Feeling good can become your new normal if you're available for it to be.

I decided to write this book for many reasons. In my twenty-year career of working with people, in facilitating healing from past pain and trauma, and witnessing change through my counseling services, advocacy work, and supporting individuals in living a better life, I have learned a lot about how self-esteem issues and lack of confidence impact women and their relationships, their money, and their overall health. On a spectrum from staying in half-ass marriages to attracting the love of your life, I've seen it all and lived it. This book is a mix of my personal experiences, wealth of education, and work experience as a counselor and coach, with a sprinkle of humor.

I believe that every woman who heals herself inside out also heals her children and her children's children and breaks generational cycles. My intention for this book is to inspire you and women like you to stop putting everyone else before yourselves. I want you to release the exhaustion in being anything but yourself and start appreciating all of the things that have shaped you and brought you to this point in time. I want you to understand the power in caring for yourself. My wish for you is that you start to prioritize how you feel. For some of you, this isn't a new concept, and for others, this will be the first time you explore what self-care really is and why it's imperative to living your healthiest and best life.

Each chapter starts off with a confession. I'm going deep. I'm airing my dirty laundry with hope that my pain, grief, heartache, mistakes, and experiences will now become another woman's tool kit. I have clung to my faith in desperation throughout many challenges in my life and vowed several times to use my experiences to help others heal and transform their lives from the inside out—*if* God carried me through the darkest days I faced alone.

He did, and so here I am, writing this book for you.

I have climbed many mountains both in a metaphoric sense and in real life. I will open up in a way I never have, in hopes that my personal stories will inspire you to persevere in your own journey to fully and completely love yourself inside out. It's definitely a process, and it starts with the decision that you want to truly connect with who you are—not who society tells you to be but who you actually are. It's time to peel the mask all the way off and get real about your life. My intention is that this book will help you unlock the inner badass and the fierce warrior woman you have been hiding from the world. I recognize that sometimes you've hidden her because you want to protect her, and other times because you're not 100 percent sure who she is. You can assess and analyze things until you are blue in the face, like Smurfette, or you can decide right now that you are done settling for anything less than your heart's desires, and you want to tap into more of what those desires are. You get to choose to let go of all the hurt, all of the heartache, all of the relationships that have eaten at you, bit by bit. You get to choose to tell a new story about your life. You are free to be whoever you want to be. You get to discover all the parts of yourself you have stuffed down, down, down, in hopes of pleasing everyone around you, while constantly disappointing yourself.

Self-reflection is a powerful tool, but rehashing your past will make you miss out on all the glorious things waiting for you to step up and into the woman God created you to be. Are you ready to dot your i's and cross your t's on your terms?

True growth comes when you learn how to make peace with your past and stay present in the now. You've heard that cliché saying that the present is a gift, and I am here to remind you that it really is. The shame, embarrassment, and anger you are carrying with you from years gone by is blocking every blessing God has planned for you. It's time to release all things weighing you down and start experiencing life on the other side of fear. I am so glad you have picked up my book. Whether you already feel good about yourself or want to feel better, this book holds something inside for you. You aren't alone, sister, and you will get through whatever you are facing. Welcome to your next breakthrough.

As a self-care junkie, I am 100 percent committed to improving myself, my communication, my relationships, my business, and everything in between.

I'm addicted to constantly working on myself and discovering more about what makes me tick. You've heard the saying—every new level you evolve to will demand a new you.

I'm addicted to researching new ideas to help me become the best me ever.

I'm addicted to personal development. It's very intrinsically rewarding to want to be kind to myself and to constantly discover new things about myself. I believe we are always evolving; we are supposed to. Growth trumps stagnancy, every time.

I am addicted to using my skills and abilities to help others heal themselves from the inside out so they too can live a life they actually want to wake up to every single day.

Transformation takes time, energy, and commitment.

I am not only addicted to reading personal development books, I'm addicted to writing them as well. This book is about self-care and what that looks like from a holistic approach.

I'm addicted to vanilla bean candles, salt lamps, and energy healing work.

I'm unapologetically addicted to drinking large quantities of water in a day (and I'm grateful to have access to clean water on the daily!).

I'm addicted to trying new foods, eating cleaner, and experimenting with exercise.

I'm addicted to pushing myself past my fear-based limits.

I'm completely hooked on anything by Abraham Hicks.

I'm addicted to learning the art of real forgiveness of self and others.

I'm addicted to owning my role in relationship breakdowns and refuse to live in victimhood.

I'm addicted to helping people like *you* invest in yourself, improve your life, and feel better in every capacity.

That's, *ahem*, why I wrote this book.

What are you addicted to?

Is it healthy, positive, and fulfilling behavior?

Or are you addicted to toxic, chaotic, unhealthy, and unfulfilling behavior or people?

I want self-care to be viewed in a holistic manner, or should I say *whole-istic*? As in, caring for all of you, from the *inside* out. From this moment forward, whatever you think you know about self-care, I ask you to open your mind up to learning more and to actually putting into practice some of the techniques and ideas written in these pages.

I want every single one of you to realize that a bubble bath is great, and dark chocolate is fantastic, but those are only surface-level means to indulge in caring for your badass self.

It's pretty straightforward, right? I mean, you shower regularly, don't you? You brush your teeth every night and chug water like it's your job after a night of too much red wine, yes? So, you're already on the right path. Let's go deeper.

Too often, women I work with, meet at events, or hear from online think self-care is limited to manicures and pedicures and negate to honor the other avenues and opportunities that it includes. The ways in which you care for yourself reflect how much you love yourself. Self-care is a term being thrown around the internet like a funny dog meme, but it really means taking care of yourself—your whole self, head to toe and all the in-betweens.

I felt called to write this book for many reasons—mostly, to use pieces of my personal life journey, education, and work experience to teach how significant self-care is and the variety of ways to actually take good care of yourself no matter what season of life you are in. I've worked in the social services field for twenty years, supporting, counseling, and coaching men and women. That's two freaking decades, people! I kept having this nudge to add to the mix of divine feminine healing in our world and to stand up and remind women everywhere that you are not your size. You are not your past. You are not the titles you wear. You are not your biggest regret. You are a powerful and capable soul who gets to decide who she is and how she lives. Sisters, you are important! No matter where you are or where you've been, you matter.

I want to bring attention to the uncommon ways we can take care of ourselves—mind, body, and soul—in the common world.

It's very interesting to me how male psychiatrists, psychologists, doctors, teachers, pastors, healers, and my fellow spiritually woke brothers stand up and speak to us, as women, about what we need to start doing and stop doing in order to feel better, and we listen closely. We literally sit on the edge of our seats, ears wide open. In fact, historically, men have been the decision makers for women's health issues. Scary!

It's like we are programmed to cling to their every word, always being submissive. I believe their intentions are good, their information is super valuable, and I trust that we as a society do need great men talking about self-care and growth. It's a beautiful thing. Truly, it is …

But—and this is a big *but*! I believe that now more than ever, we need you, our fellow sisters, to rise up, to allow yourselves to be seen and heard. We need to hear your stories and to learn from your experiences. Women, you have been called to lead in a way you've never done before. It's time to start tapping into your spiritual gifts and teaching from your truths. We need to learn from one another. We need to universally respect one another and embrace our differences, all while recognizing that at our core, we are all divinely loved and worthy.

We need to embrace our uniqueness as women and celebrate our divine femininity while we recognize and appreciate how we are different from men. Your time is now. You are the woman who will help transform our world for generations to follow. Women who lead, I see you. I honor you. I know it hasn't been easy, yet here you stand. You are magnificent in all your glory. You are a warrior; it doesn't matter who knows your story. You know your truth. It is time to speak it.

We know that, as women, we were created to be different, not the exact same. We deserve to honor our inner feminine goddess. We need to be in community with one another. Women supporting women will change the world. We get to break the stereotypes that women are catty gossips and drama queens. We get to show the people in our circle how great life flows when we work together and celebrate one another.

I want every single person in the entire world to love and accept themselves. For the sake of this book, I am speaking directly to you, my fellow woman—sister, mother, grandmother, aunt, cousin, friend.

This book is designed to take you from chaos to clarity; from self-sabotaging to self-care; from fearful to free.

Taking care of yourself is your responsibility, and if I may be so bold, it needs to be your first priority. I'm talking about all the things—spiritually, mentally, physically, sexually, emotionally, and financially.

Life experiences shape us, of course, but it's our job to figure out what we need to stop doing and what we need to start doing in order to feel our best. We have to learn how to parent ourselves and stop blaming the ones who raised us, no matter how great or not so great they were. We've got to cut the cords attached to the hurt and pain we have survived and start living in the present moment—the here and now.

Most importantly, you have to stop looking for someone to do it for you.

You cannot be saved by anyone but your own self.

We have to figure out what we need in order to become who we want to be so that we can live the life we desire. We've got to stop using wine, chocolate, Ambien, or bath bombs to get through the day and instead learn how to fulfill our emotional needs. Instead of getting buzzed up on sugar or any other available substance to escape our pain, frustration, or whatever it is we want to avoid dealing with, we must adult like it's our full-time job (because it is!) and indulge in those things as a means to enjoy our lives, to enhance our lives, not to *get us through* life.

I have had the privilege of working with thousands of fellow humans, helping them heal from pain and turn it into purposeful living. Through the power of self-acceptance, we can create our lives in a way that feels good by understanding who we are and how we need to care for ourselves in order to show up as our best selves. We need to cut through our own bullshit.

I want to teach you how to intentionally create the life you want to wake up to every single day and how to move through life with confidence.

Talking about self-care is similar to talking about sex. It's considered taboo and even selfish by some, weird or uncomfortable by others, and yet you're expected to know what to do. It's like a first-time mom; she goes through her pregnancy, gives birth, then boom! She's taking her baby home, and she's got to figure out what her little human needs depending on which cry is happening. And then of course she's also responsible for the laundry, the meals, the grocery shopping, the other family members, and remembering Aunt Rita's birthday. I mean, c'mon now. What isn't highlighted and written in stone upon discharge from the hospital is how imperative it is that she take care of herself first. That she heals. That means eating, sleeping as much as possible, recovering *down there*, and—oh my Lanta!—yes, asking for help and delegating tasks to her partner or other family members and friends.

But that's not specifically what this book is all about really. This book is about making the decision to prioritize yourself—period. To stop living under the constraints of others and to free yourself from the negative feelings, fears, and doubts keeping you up at night.

It's full of tidbits of my personal stories, life experiences, and all the things that guided me to do the very same thing. I share some uncomfortable things from my past that allowed me to get intentional about my health, my money, and essentially my quality of life.

Throughout these pages, you'll be inspired to tap into your own superpowers, intuition, and desires and leverage your personality to work for you.

I want to teach you that self-care is more about taking responsibility for your life than it is about drowning in chocolate. It's about owning your desires, needs, and asserting yourself in all capacities and relationships, and it does in fact include having great sex. It also includes calling yourself out on your own stuff and pointing your finger at yourself, not everybody else.

Self-care is as much about checking in with yourself and being accountable for getting your life together as it is prioritizing alone time, pampering yourself, and learning how to effectively destress, all while managing the chaotic moments (and people).

I believe in a holistic approach to wellness—mind, body, soul. I practice this in my own life and have taught thousands of clients this concept.

Years ago, when I would use the term *self-care*, especially in a presentation or while speaking at a conference, people would roll their eyes at me. It was considered taboo to teach people, specifically women, that saying no was important, that taking care of their health was important, and heaven forbid if I dared encourage a woman to clock out at lunch and not eat at her desk.

I will say things have come along way over the years, but now we are in such a mental health crisis it's absurd. If more people would accept that prioritizing your needs is critical to your overall health and wellness, I trust things would be different. I bet many of you practice self-care in different ways but don't label it as such. Some of my stories may resonate with you, and some may not. Take what you need and leave the rest behind.

The easier you choose to let *being you* be, the easier life gets.

The more compassion you have with yourself, the healthier and lighter you will feel.

Ready to finally reconnect with yourself? To heal your relationship with your body? Change your money story and financial experience? Ready to reclaim your health? Reclaim your voice? Take back your power? Completely shift the momentum in your life? That is what this book is all about.

Are you ready to unleash the woman who has been waiting for this moment, to stand up and be seen and heard? She's on the perch, ready to be set free. She's ready to open her wings and fly.

Will you let her fly free? Allow her to leave the cage she's been trapped in for so many years?

Today, your life is forever changed. There is no going back now, gorgeous! I'm so excited for you to transform your love story with yourself. You are the hero in your own life. It is safe for you to be seen and heard in this world. Welcome to your transformation. Get in the driver's seat and buckle up, baby. It's prime time to shine. Start the car and hit the gas! There's no going back now. Everything that has brought you to this moment is all just dust in your rearview mirror now. You've turned the corner and squealed the tires. It's time for you to honor your truth and to no longer abandon yourself or your desires.

These are my confessions … (Cue the Usher song!)

COMMITMENT TO SELF-CARE

In my experience, declaring your goals, intentions, and commitments out loud makes a big difference. You deserve to experience life free from past pain, filled with gratitude, and feeling your best. Below is your commitment statement. Your declaration for yourself to yourself. A reminder of what you signed up for when you bought my book. A vow that holds so much love and power. A commitment to self-care. A commitment to you, Goddess.

I,_____, commit to loving myself, honoring myself, trusting myself, and caring for myself in all that I say, all that I do, and all that I am.

I am no longer available for_____
_____
_____
_____

I am totally open to and available for_____
_____
_____
_____

Signed this date_____

My mission is to impact millions of people to believe in themselves.
—*PRIMETIME Success*

SPIRITUAL SELF-CARE

CHAPTER 1

Confession: I Never Listen to the Neighbors

It was a wintery day in October in the late seventies when the cutest and most precious little girl came into the world. She was full of life and touched everyone's heart on the third floor, also known as obstetrics. It was Halloween day, and the weather was cold and snowy, so bundled up snug as a bug in a rug, her mother and father loaded her up and headed for home. A peaceful sleeping beauty, she looked almost like a doll, minus the hair. New life and new possibilities at her fingertips. Adventures ahead of her that no one would predict. Yes, that sweet, innocent little bundle of love is writing this book. I'm talking about myself, so I may be a tad biased about how darn cute I was, but I've got the baby pictures to prove it.

According to my mother, I was a very happy baby. Feed me, cuddle me, and let me sleep; that's all I needed. I guess some things never change! Little did I know that the following eighteen years would be full of extreme highs and lows that would challenge me, change me, and allow me to have a great opportunity to help other people navigate the journey of stepping into who God called them to be. Above the circumstances you have faced, beyond the limitations that authority figures try to put on you, and with more belief in yourself and conviction in your deservingness, you will do the great things you dream of doing. Building a solid foundation to stand on and using your voice and raising your hand is where next-level self-care begins.

I learned around age eight or nine that I had been an accident. My mother and father were not enjoying married life together, and things were not going well. Hello! Then I came along. I have always known since that time that God had big plans for my life. I firmly believe that planned children are wonderful, but a lot of times, it is those of us who were not expected who change the world. It's like the big guy works his magic and destines us to be born.

When you're born, you are a helpless bundle of innocent, pure love. It's such a wonderful fact that no matter which family you are born into, you have a purpose for your life, your existence. You were created for greatness—whatever that is for you. Some of you can relate to struggling to discover what that is much more than others. You, of course, don't know what your purpose in life is until you explore the possibilities, your interests, and your skills and talents and tune into your intuition. It's a total discovery process with a lot of ups and downs. When you're little, the people around you think they know what you are destined to become. Your parents have opinions, your siblings have opinions, the neighbors have opinions, and anyone else in your immediate circle surely has a comment or two about what you will do or who you will be as you grow. As hours turn into days, and days into weeks, and weeks into months, and months into years, your personality shines through, and again there are different opinions about you and your destiny. It's inevitable. It's how it goes. Some people never really figure it out, and others fulfill their destiny. I always knew I would be an author. As a former spelling bee champion, county public-speaking-contest winner, and writing-contest champ, it surely is my calling in this world. Just saying!

Which category are you in right now? Do you know what your calling in life is?

When you do figure out who you are and tap into your greater purpose, your life starts to flow effortlessly and magically in ways you cannot imagine right now if you are stuck in resistance or in the opinions of other people. Figuring that out takes a lot of work, self-discovery, and a commitment to being yourself. You must learn how to tap into your intuition. There are signs, whispers, songs, and many other ways infinite intelligence is communicating to you. Your job is to figure out what is being said. Don't worry! It's only taken me thirty-plus years! Don't give up if you feel confused about your life, work, and purpose. We all start out in this world with a dozen or more people who, perhaps well intentioned, tell us what and who we are. "Oh, you look just like Aunt Shirley; those cheekbones were meant to be on a magazine cover!" or "You have the personality and patience of Aunt Patty; you're going to be a teacher just like she was!" or "You're going to be a farmwife like Grandma because you've got her fingers; ain't nobody able to peel potatoes like Grandma!" You get the drift, right? We get confusing information about who we are supposed to be in our adult life based on the projections and opinions of those around us as we are growing up. We also carry with us programmed patterns of behavior that we learned throughout our childhood. If you act a certain way, you'll get your parents' approval. If you falter, then you've lost it. You have been conditioned to behave in certain ways in different environments and around certain people.

The great news is that as you grow and mature, you get to take full responsibility of your life, patterns, and programming and change it all. We have to learn how to separate our goals and hearts' desires from those projections and suggestions in order to step into who we fully and truly are. It takes a whole lot of guts, self-awareness, time, and work. One of the best ways to tune into your innate calling is to pay attention to what lights your soul on fire. When do you feel your best? What makes you stand on your soapbox and never want to step down? Those kinds of questions lead to clarity. A big part of your responsibility is to tune out the opinions of the people around you and ask yourself what you love to do.

As a young girl, I remember feeling so different from everybody. I was the girl who, as the neighbors put it, came from a broken family. My father and mother separated and divorced when I was two. I grew up without my biological father in the picture, other than the odd sighting and stare down at Towers (now known as Zellers). I felt the stigma everywhere I went. I was adopted at the age of eleven, and I was sixteen before I called the man who raised me Dad. I feel strongly that who you are and who you were born to be is a lot more about discovering your spiritual gifts than your DNA. I only know pieces about my DNA—more specifically, the pieces I have been told. I am living proof that no matter where you came from, you can be whoever you want to be. You just have to decide who that is and become that person.

Can you imagine what it was like to be a child living in a small village where everybody knew everybody, and then within twenty-four hours, you one day have a different name? Especially at the tween stage of your life? It was an experience I have never forgotten. The whole thing went down like this: I went to school and came home as usual. I waited for my parents to get home, and then we drove twenty-five minutes to a sketchy building in a nearby city. We went into an office area inside of the building, where I had to sit in a tiny little room on a stinky, old couch, directly across from my biological father, who I'd never met and had zero relationship with. He didn't say a word to me. He stared like a deer caught in headlights as a lawyer and some children's services person asked him if he understood that signing his rights over to my new dad meant he was no longer responsible for me. Talk about a total punch to the gut. Wow! Back up the bus! Those words rattled me for many years. I never really let on that they did because it was clear to me early on that I was a rock for my family. That was my role. I was the child who was always *fine*. The child who would be seen and not heard, and so long as I operated that way, everything else would be *fine*.

Recalling that moment in my life makes me shake my head, literally!

The way it all went down was so traumatic and unhealthy, but that's how child services rolled back then. Have they improved much since? That's debatable.

I remember getting a gold Avon XOXO pinky ring (which I still have), going out for dinner, and then going home and straight to bed. There was no heehaw celebration like you see in the movies. It was what it was, and that's all that it was, but it was everything to me. I recall waking up the next day wondering why I didn't feel different. Wasn't my whole world supposed to change once I finally had the same name as my mother? I mean, that was the biggest joke going. I was teased all the time by jerks at school and at church about that. Didn't my value and worth go up overnight because I was no longer in a "broken" family?

As I got off the school bus and entered the school, I remember feeling extreme embarrassment. Here I was telling the bus driver, the custodian, and any person who'd listen all about my name change and how I now had a real dad, but the kids at school were cruel. They hadn't come from that kind of situation. They didn't get it, and their parents probably told them we were the weird family because back then—believe it or not—women stayed in nasty marriages and situations because they were afraid of what people would say. So, Momma! I'm proud of you for doing what you had to do no matter what the church ladies whispered about you, and I'm happy that you had the ovaries to go against the sad norm at that time in history. It doesn't matter what the relationship story is, all that matters is when a woman is unhappy or unhealthy, she makes a decision to change.

Printing out a new last name on my schoolwork was the easy part. I felt like such a badass. Do you remember when you were younger, doodling your crush's name with yours? You know what I mean, don't you? When you think you're in love with the boy who sits across from you in the desk with all the chewed-off pencils? You take your doodling one step further and practice writing your name adding his last name, right? I had practiced writing out my new last name for a good solid year or two before it became my reality. My mother had remarried in the late eighties. I was adopted in the early nineties. Proof! You can write your life into existence. I learned that lesson when I was young and way before any law of attraction books were known to me, let alone available to me. I had zero information about universal laws at that time in my life.

Moving forward, I pray the education system has changed because as I was skipping along the hallways and out to my class portable, thinking life was great, better than good, the teachers kept referring to me as my former surname, which was French, and they couldn't pronounce it correctly to begin with. I knew it wasn't just my imagination; my life had changed overnight, yet I was still so invisible. Most of the teachers were insensitive and probably needed what today would be called sensitivity training. There are so many different types of families nowadays that things must have evolved. As I wrote about those memories, it dawned on me that compassion wasn't really a thing, back then. There were no participation ribbons, no equality in classrooms, and no trauma educators or counselors floating through the halls. That is the norm now. Children are no longer expected to just disappear into their pain or fear. They get to have a voice. They get to be seen and heard. They get to be celebrated.

I ran into the classroom portable where my grade-five teacher was preparing for the day ahead. I enthusiastically told her that I had a new name because I had been adopted the night prior. I was feeling proud. I finally had the same last name as my mother. I asked my teacher to please call me by my new name, and guess what she did? That not-so-softhearted Ukrainian teacher looked at me like I was crazy. I remember feeling crushed. The teacher's reaction caused emotional scarring that took a long time to process and heal. I valued her opinion because I respected her as my teacher. I had a fleeting thought of reaching out to her while writing this book. I decided I have come too far in my own growth to reopen that door, and really, would she care? Then I thought perhaps she isn't even alive anymore. Who knows? All I know is that teachers have a profound and powerful influence on their students and need to be aware of that at all times and in all situations. You listening, teach? Sidenote: I married a teacher. He was in the profession for all the right reasons, but I digress.

So, there I was. Eleven. My identity had changed with a new surname, yet I still had no clue who I was. But what I did know was that I was still invisible to the people who I wanted to see me. I looked in the mirror and saw the same person, but I felt different now. Was it finally happening? Was I normal now? Was this how it was supposed to feel to have two parents? Was I worthy now of being accepted among my peers? I experienced many emotions in that first month—embarrassment, confusion, excitement, anger, and ultimately a sense of fear. Since it had become official, I had all sorts of questions racing around my mind. What if my new dad left too? Would I have to go back to my original name? Would he like having a daughter? Would I be good enough to make him stay? What if he and my mother got divorced? What if he thought children were a nuisance? Although these questions sound sad and scary for an eleven-year-old girl to ponder, and they were, it was my reality at the time, and I legitimately thought that if I misbehaved in any way, my new dad would leave. I knew what the spoken and unspoken expectations were in our household, and I did my best to be obedient. A *good* Baptist girl. There were a lot of things going on in our house, but the neighbors never noticed.

I wanted the same name as my mother for years, and when it happened, it was super stressful. I mean, I finally belonged in a weird and messed-up way to what was a socially acceptable family. Keep in mind that these things (being a blended family and being adopted by your mom's husband) were unheard of in the little village I was raised in. I was, by all means, the girl who was never going to make it, according the neighbors. *I never listen to the neighbors.* I didn't then, and I don't now. It's a personal policy. Other people's opinions are none of my business. I learned that decades ago and have been speaking that truth ever since.

I was sixteen before I addressed my dad as such. I'd always called him by his first name because I hadn't been directed to do otherwise. He was, in essence, my dad long before I said the title. He chose to step up and take responsibility for me, to love me unconditionally, and to teach me all about life in the best way he could. I loved that man and feared him at the same time. He was a force to be reckoned with. He was a kind and intelligent man to most. Looking back, those years were building great resilience in me and have had a significant impact on who I am as a woman and as a mother. It's interesting to reflect back on that season of my life. When I thought about all of the reasons I am the woman I am today, it was clear that my identity has shifted and evolved over the years, which is what is supposed to happen as we grow. We have been created for a purpose, perhaps more than one.

Some of you may be questioning your purpose right now. Figuring it out gets to be fun. It is a part of your evolution—the knowing. I know for a fact that everything happens for a reason. My dad needed to be there for me even though he wasn't there when I was created. It was God's plan. I may not have had his eyes or smile, but I definitely had his heart. As sentimental as I am, I do not exclude the struggles from my gratitude list. Every difficult event I went through, that we went through as a family, allowed me to expand. There were many awkward stages, as one would expect when blending families. Awkward and out of place had become my normal though, so essentially, it felt familiar.

I knew the adoption and name change was weird for my friends because all of them lived with their biological parents, and no one spoke of divorce, let alone stepfamilies. It was something reserved for *bad* Christians. As time went on, it became more normal to others, but inside my head, I always struggled with who I was and why God brought me into the world. I often wondered why having two parents created such discourse inside of me? Wasn't I supposed to feel safe in our home? What was my purpose? Why did I exist? How could I be the girl my heart screamed at me to be in the face of adversity? Why did I love and fear the same person? What was all the adversity the neighbors talked about around me? Why didn't any of them jump in and help us out as a family if they were concerned? Answers I've accepted that I'll never have and no longer have any attachment to.

I have a deep appreciation for my upbringing. I am who I am because of all the things I have gone through, and I am more resilient than most, as a result. I look at everything as an opportunity for growth. My parents taught me about many positive things like: strong work ethic, and the importance of giving back to my community through volunteering. They did a lot of volunteer work. It really does take a village. My parents got me involved with organizations and clubs. They thought it would be good for me to go away to Girl Guide camps every summer. I did learn a lot of useful life skills and have no issue being alone. My dad signed me up for the 4-H club because it was important that girls knew they could do things that boys did. Those were the days! Roll call! (I have my 4-H Member sign in our garage.) My dad was a firefighter for nearly three decades. He was always demonstrating leadership, service, and the commitment to helping others. I pretty much grew up at the firehall. I was so proud of him. When it was time for bed and he wasn't home from a fire call, I would try so hard to stay awake so I could hear when he returned. I needed to know he was safe and that everything was okay. When you're a young child and your parent has a responsibility like firefighters do, you worry.

I believe that my parents did the best they could with the knowledge they had. And I'm grateful to God every day that my dad was my dad no matter how it all had to happen. My dad and I were always close, and we developed an out-of-this-world relationship once I became an adult. I love him very much and always will. He passed away in November 2014 with family surrounding him. I carry his love with me just like that George Strait song. My dad was a good man who lived one hell of a life, and he tried to do the best he could to raise me, a daughter who wasn't his responsibility. He truly stepped up even though he didn't have to. Some people say blood is thicker than water, but I disagree. Love is stronger than blood. Do you agree?

My dad was the most incredible grandfather to my son and helped me in so many ways when later in life I became a single mother. He was reliable, always—something a lot of men throughout my life have never been.

I choose gratitude. I choose forgiveness. I choose love. He taught me those things. Essentially, he taught me how to be a badass. He would always say, "Be kind but take no sh*t."

I learned so much about who I am as a woman because of the differences and difficulties I went through in my childhood. What used to make me feel weary and insecure now allows me to help so many other people. If I'm completely honest with you—which, hello, this book is about confessions—I realized many years ago that biological families equaling less dysfunction is a myth. I know people who have been born and raised in their biological family homes who have more issues than I ever could. Perception, y'all.

I am who I am because of the course my life took, and I wouldn't change it for a minute. Transformation is possible, and wisdom can only come from experience.

The significance of this particular chapter in initiating what I intend to be a completely open-minded perspective on self-care and the importance of it in all areas of life is to point attention to how critical it is to know thy self. You may be familiar with that ancient Greek aphorism. Self-care comes from a place of love for yourself. When you love yourself, no matter what or who you used to be, you are on your way to living a great life. Maybe you have a story similar to mine. Perhaps you have a completely different experience. Either way, it doesn't matter. You are not destined to live in your past. You are a creative soul on a journey from then to now, and you must trust that things continue to get better and better for you, because they will.

I believe our childhoods shape us. That's their purpose. It is all preparation for our adult years and not an excuse to be a victim or a miserable person. You get to choose your attitude, and it has nothing to do with your past. You don't know it when you're young, but you have so much more potential than what you imagine you do in fifth grade.

I had to decide who I was and figure it out independently because my identity was up in the air for so long. I had to sort out who I was as a young girl, as a teenager (scary years), and the woman I have become today. It's a process. I believe that we can be whoever we want to be if we work at becoming *her* no matter where we come from. Start to imagine what kind of life you want to live and ask yourself, Who do you need to be in order to experience it? Do not let your childhood or your current situation dictate who you have to be and instead start making conscious choices about your life. You are not what people say you are. You are whoever you say you are.

Some of you are desperate to figure out who you are. Not because you were adopted, per se, but because you're feeling lost. You aren't clear on your purpose. You've associated your identity with the titles placed upon you and the opinions of others. It becomes confusing at times when you start to heal parts of yourself and strip off the labels other people have given you about who you are or what you should be doing with your life. I empathize with you. I have been there, a few times! It gets confusing because most of our lives, we are told who we are supposed to be by everybody around us, including societal conditioning, the beauty industry, and lifestyle marketing tactics. Our personality, looks, self-esteem, and beliefs shape our identity. As you mature and develop your own sense of self, things will change, and you'll start questioning everything you once thought you knew about yourself, your relationships, your belief systems, and all the other things in between.

Until you make a decision to get intentional about your life, you will waffle between being who people expect you to be or know you to be and who you want to be and feel called to be. It's an uncomfortable growth spurt. You will have to accept that and move forward.

When was the last time you questioned who you are and what your next move needs to be? Do you make decisions from a place of confidence or insecurity? What outdated beliefs are you carrying around with you about who you are based on your past?

What new beliefs would you like to hold?

People think what they want to think, and they will believe what they choose to, whether it's true or not. It's time to stop living your life on the sideline, waiting for the whistle to blow before you press play on your dreams. You'll never impress everybody, and quite frankly, why would you want to? It's not your responsibility to prove your worth or to live on someone else's terms or timeline. Self-care involves respecting yourself, owning who you are, and not apologizing for it. No more catering to other people's opinions about your life, okay? It is not your responsibility to fulfill other people's expectations. That doesn't mean you quit on your responsibilities and commitments to others, but it does mean you live in accordance with your core values and function from a place of personal integrity. You are so much more than you give yourself credit for, and you are not the titles you wear.

Today, I want you to look at yourself in the mirror, put your hand on your heart, and promise to be true to yourself. Promise to be gentler with yourself and to treat yourself with compassion. Ask for guidance and be open to receiving it. Commit to loving yourself as you are and, in this moment, declare your worthiness to have everything you have dreamed of and more. It is time to unleash your inner badass. She's ready to shine brighter than ever. You get to decide who you are. You are so much greater than the titles you wear: mom, wife, sister, daughter, auntie, boss, employee, chauffeur, chef, accountant, coach, volunteer, and so on. Those titles are not *who* you are; they are pieces of who you are and things that you do or have done. You were someone before all of those titles were put on you, so your job is to decide who you want to be at your core and be *her*. Don't worry about what the neighbors say.

A Prayer for Guidance

Dear God, I am feeling confused right now about who you desire me to be. Please show me how you want me to live and how you desire me to serve you and others. I am open to receiving your signs and guidance as I take responsibility to fulfill my destiny. Thank you for shining your light and unconditional love on my life. I am ready to live differently. Amen.

CHAPTER 2

Confession: I Was Searching for a Guru in All the Wrong Places

It was 2013, and the copywriter I'd hired to create some headlines, opt-ins, and taglines for my social media and website kept referring to me as Christy the Guru. I remember feeling flattered yet weird. Me, a guru? I'd never thought of myself as such. I remember messaging back and forth on Facebook messenger and telling her to refrain from using the label *Guru* on my site and in my copy. Stunned, she inquired about why I felt that way because she looked at me as a guru. I was wise, a mix of both the school of hard knocks and academia, yes, but I was a woman, like all of you, trying to keep my head above water. Dodging whatever raising a teenager would throw at me, running a business that hadn't yet made much money, and living the wifey life. When she asked me how I had become so successful, it made me acknowledge all of the work I'd done to transform my entire identity. I recognized something important at that point. I was the guru I was looking for. Well, my higher self was. I sat in awe for at least twenty minutes. Nobody had ever really inquired about my success journey. I was raised that it is rude to toot your own horn. I started to toot it. I ran to the mirror, looked deep into my eyes, and cried. "You did this," I whispered to myself. "You made this transformation." Pass the Kleenex, please.

People only ever focused on my external transformations. You know, if I'd gained or lost weight, if I cut or colored my hair, all the things they could physically see. As I received her sweet and factual compliment, I gave praise to God. I had been through a lot at that point in my life and had worked extremely hard on releasing preconceived notions about who I was, healing myself, releasing old heartache, and forgiving myself and others for a variety of things. I spent many years lost in prayer, begging God to help me through situations with the promise that if he did, I would forever use my strength and wisdom to teach women around the world how to heal and transform their lives from the inside out too. I believe that we go through things in order to help others who will go through similar things. I also acknowledge that when we are struggling and hurting, we too can be a source of pain for others. We must own our role in relationships and accept responsibility accordingly. Does that mean we have to like the depths of pain or loss we experience? Absolutely not. Does it mean that we stay stuck in guilt or shame for behaving in a way that was less than desirable? Not at all. It does mean that we move through forgiveness for ourselves with others and start looking at situations with compassion and an open mind. When we grow through what we go through, we possess the skills and experience to help others, and that is a beautiful gift to give.

Think about difficult situations you have survived and come out the other side from. How can you help others with that knowledge and wisdom you now carry as a result of it? When you reframe your thoughts from *why did that happen to me* to *how may I help another going through it,* your energy shifts, and your heart feels lighter. It takes away some of the heaviness we tend to carry when we have gone through pain and loss. There is so much power in transforming our experiences into being the light for others. There are moments when we have all searched outside of ourselves for answers that only we hold within ourselves. It happens. We figure it out and move forward. There is nothing to feel ashamed about, and there is no reason to perpetuate that pattern. Acknowledge it and release it.

Free yourself from the expectation that you have to know it all right now, and focus on discovering more about yourself on this incredible life journey.

Back in 2013, everyone and their sister was self-labeling themselves a guru of this and that, and it drove me bananas. It irked me for many reasons, mostly because I have always trusted and believed that nobody can tell us what we need more precisely than our intuition and source connection. When we turn to God and pray it out, trusting that the solution will be made available to us or the insight will be given, we shift from a panic state to one of ease and comfort. It is safe to release control over your problems. It is safe to surrender. Albeit, at times you don't like the answer or the actions required, or you struggle to be still and quiet long enough to hear the message. If you develop a spiritual practice, one that works for you and your belief system, it will be an incredible support system for you. Spiritual self-care at its finest. If you do not believe in anything, how will you ever get through difficult times? Where will you put your trust and hope for better days?

Back in 2013, I hadn't matured enough in my spiritual journey to realize that of course God created gurus, or in-tune healers, as I refer to them, to help others along their own journey. It would be common knowledge to me now, but as we grow, we learn more about what is possible and what is true. With all of that being said, please excuse me for searching outside of myself for a period of time. I'll explain.

Things shifted a bit when I was introduced to a well-respected holistic nutritionist who quickly told me I needed to book an appointment with her to figure out why I was having some odd health ailments. How did she know? We were complete strangers, and then it clicked! I'd been praying for God to guide me to the person who could help me. Things do not just happen out of the blue, although it can feel that way sometimes. There is always a reason. Always. Even if we don't understand it at the time. I have always been a believer in a very unorganized way although I was raised in organized religion. I turned to God so many times throughout my childhood that I *know,* for me personally, he is real. Very real. God within us and God outside of us. Call it Source, call it Creator, call it Infinite Intelligence. It is real. I would not be here writing this book if I had not built my relationship with source. In many instances throughout my life, when I felt so alone and had no one to talk to, I prayed. I talked to God. I didn't know it would be labelled self-care to have a spiritual practice three and a half decades ago, but I was doing it as young as I can remember. I continued to, and my spiritual connection is healthier than it has ever been. It was truly my only saving grace—prayer and having someone to call Father years ago when I felt abandoned and lost. When you grow up fatherless, you find a way to survive. Mine was faith. Maybe you are struggling in your relationship with God right now because of circumstances, loss, or other things. I can relate. Many situations and losses in my life have caused me to want to turn my back on God because I just didn't or don't understand why! Yet, throughout all of my trials and tribulations, the only consistent thing in my life has been God and my ability to talk to him, angry or with a happy heart. He is there to turn to. It may sound cliché, but it's true. At least it's my truth. You'll have to figure out what your truth is.

As a result of that interaction with the holistic nutritionist, I started to focus on my gut health. I have extensive education in developmental disabilities and mental health, so understanding the significance of what we eat and our digestive health was not new to me. I began to experience mild relief. I would go to each appointment asking the same questions: What is happening to me? What blocks must I clear? Why is my neck so tight? Why is one side of my face numb? Why is my vision blurry? Why are my ears ringing, and why aren't the green juices helping? She would look at me and say, "You know why." I would leave there so frustrated. I'd mutter to myself all the way from the elevator to the parking lot, "Duh, if I knew why, I'd figure out how to fix it." Then I'd return a week or two later.

I was so focused on what was happening to me and fighting to keep my head above water because my responsibilities as a wife, mother, and business owner hadn't disappeared. There's a major question I never asked, and that was, "What is the lesson I need to learn?" I'd forgotten that trusting myself was the answer. That's a whole other book, but seriously, there is always a lesson. I knew it then, and I know it now. I quite simply got lost in the symptoms I was experiencing and forgot. Have you ever been so fixated on your *symptoms* in health, in relationships, and in work struggles that you overlooked the message? Symptoms can be chest pain, poor sleep, unnecessary worry or fear, headaches, pretty much anything that causes a distraction from the root issue.

Our bodies communicate to us all the time; it's only a matter of whether or not we are listening to what we need to hear. If you ever struggle with joint pain, tension headaches, vertigo, or other things, be still and ask yourself what your body is trying to tell you. If you listen, your body will tell you. I have such a different perspective on life with chronic, unexplained pain symptoms. I know I had to go through those years of struggle to better understand life through that lens. It sucked. I refused pain medication, which, if I'm honest, was being offered to me by every doctor and friend I knew. I went through quite a few energy healers and a lot of money during that season in my life. I was spending hundreds of dollars a month, which soon turned to thousands. Looking back, I knew that the answer was mismanaged grief, but did I listen to my intuition? No! I bought the lie for a brief moment in time that I needed someone to tell me what was going on with me. That was the most familiar feeling as I transitioned from little girl to teenager to young woman. I was always looking outside of myself for approval and for direction on who I was and if I was living in accordance with others' comfort zones.

What a major eye roll. I was avoiding coming into direct contact with the gut-wrenching pain of watching my dad be sick for so many years and ultimately watching him take his last breath.

I have learned to become so grateful for that experience because if I hadn't gone through all of that, I wouldn't have learned the valuable lessons that I now preach and teach to anyone who will listen. The right side of the body is masculine (father) energy, and the left side is feminine (mother) energy. Pay attention to any pain symptoms or irritation and dig deeper. Every symptom presented itself on the right side of my body. If I had tuned into that earlier, my understanding wouldn't be as strong. I would not have the same wisdom I now hold. The symptoms had presented themselves a few years before my dad passed away and progressively got worse and worse leading up to his death. What I now know to be true is that the longer you avoid looking at your emotional health and relationships, the more you prolong your healing and relief of symptoms. Also, wine doesn't mask emotional pain; it only makes it worse. Cheers!

I took it on as my mission to tell every medical expert, who may or may not have had any conscious awareness of energy and vibration and soul impact, that I needed to have my chakras balanced and a good cry. Believe me when I say they thought I'd lost my mind.

As a result of my continued pain symptoms and avoidance of feeling my feelings (because I was *fine*), I desperately tried a variety of holistic remedies, essential oils, nutritional supplements, and more emotion-based journaling. Eventually, I started to experience some relief. I realized the power of my own self, my own body at a cellular level, and how phenomenal it is. I shifted from focusing solely on the symptoms to focusing on feeling better. I refused to take any prescription medications, so the support of a non-energy healer went to the curb, and thankfully this journey led me to a greater self-awareness and trust that I am my own guru. Isn't it ironic how we are taught to ignore our gut instincts and do as we are told as we're growing up, and only when we tune into our gut are we on our way to healthier living?

There is something so powerful and intrinsically rewarding to unapologetically acknowledge and own your gifts, wisdom, and experiences. We all possess the ability to heal our bodies through thoughts and visualization exercises, alongside taking action. I began to study Dr. Joe Dispenza a few years ago, and the transformations I have been experiencing are mind-blowing. Between his teachings and those of the late Louise Hay, my life has changed in ways beyond my wildest dreams. I have a renewed sense of appreciation for my body and for my abilities to nourish my soul to generate great health in all areas of my life.

Developing and maintaining a spiritual practice for me is like eating a healthy diet. We nourish our bodies with food in the same way that our source connection nourishes our souls. You know more about yourself than anyone could possibly ever know. Trust that and start to listen more closely to your body. Be open to hearing the messages God sends you. It's so important as you mature in your spiritual growth to be a willing servant, and that includes the willingness to take care of yourself first. We must learn how to tune in and listen to our inner voice, but in no way, shape, or form do we have to do it alone. There are gifted healers out there, and there is a time and place for you to seek the one for you for various needs, but recognize your innate gift of knowing yourself on such a deep and connected spiritual level and stop looking for a guru to heal you. Become your own guru.

When you learn to tune in and truly listen to your intuition—a.k.a. your gut—you start to get intimate with your inner being. You will connect with yourself on a level you have never known before. One of the most loving ways you can create this connection is to stand in front of a mirror. Look deep into your eyes and tell yourself you are worthy. You are beautiful. You trust yourself. You are safe. Do this every day and as often as possible. If it feels odd at first, keep doing it. Your eyes are the window of your soul. This, my beloved goddess, is the meeting you've been waiting for, and what a beautiful meeting, indeed. You are the guru you are searching for. Yes, you! Smile because, girl, *you* have found your guru.

Clink, clink, pop! That's something worth celebrating!

A Prayer for Guidance

Dear God, thank you for the ability to forgive myself and accept myself as I am. Please help me tap into my intuition so that I can hear my own voice more clearly. I am ready to trust myself more, and I willingly accept responsibility for my life and the decisions I make. I pray this, believing you will guide me. Amen.

CHAPTER 3

Confession: I Had to Learn How to Say Au Revoir

As a young girl, I often struggled with feeling left behind. I'm not talking about FOMO, fear of missing out, which is all the craze nowadays; I'm talking about not being included in anything because nobody liked me. I was weird. I didn't fit in with the other children. I had a mushroom cut and wore Northern Reflections corduroys. In addition to those things, most of my peers bored me. I wanted to sing, dance, and do things. I did not want to feel bored. I had a big imagination. I wanted to be free. I wanted to spend recess lying in the grass, watching the clouds roll by. I wanted to talk about poems and books. Even as a young girl, I enjoyed the company of adults more than my peers. I wanted to listen to adult conversations; they were not boring.

Do you remember the days in elementary school when the teacher would say, "Pick a partner," and although you crossed your fingers, nobody called your name? Or everyone in your class had to stand on the side, and two of your peers were chosen as captains in gym class, to pick their teams, and you were always last to be called? Add to that, when you were called, it wasn't because they wanted to choose you; it was more of you were the last one standing or a better option than the other person. I have spent a great amount of time in my own head working through the thoughts and feelings that shaped my childhood. I understand now that I had low self-esteem and a desperate fear of being abandoned, but as a young child, I had no idea what caused those dark, scary, and lonesome thoughts inside of me.

A lot of those experiences are correlated to being raised without knowing my father, yes. Much more of it can be pinpointed to not knowing why. That was the question that lurked over my head for many years. Why didn't he fight for me? Why didn't he want me?

It was awkward to always be chosen last and to feel like I didn't fit in with anyone—not even my own family at times. Do not fret. I am not stuck in that place now and haven't been for a long time. It is a nauseating desire to feel wanted, which is dangerous, really, because the extreme desire to be wanted led me on a path to being wanted by all the wrong people. I digress.

When we long to feel wanted, we do things that are out of alignment with who we are. The feeling of not being wanted eats at you from the inside out until you become aware of it.

The addiction to feeling wanted trickled its way into many different relationships throughout my life, to be honest. Perhaps you can relate?

As a result of all of the unexpressed inner pain and confusion I experienced growing up, I overcompensated in pretty much all of my relationships. It usually looked like this: the female friends I had used me as the butt of their jokes, and the guys I liked didn't want a full-on relationship, but they did want access to me whenever they wanted. As I got older, and started dating, I allowed toxic men to linger around my myspace, then messenger, or in my text messages long after our time together had been exhausted. It showed up as a "Hey! How have you been?" And it quickly would escalate to "What are you wearing?" I mean, come on, dude!

Frankly, I spent so many years trying to fit in and be liked by all the wrong guys that when I had their attention, I wanted to keep it. I have great empathy and compassion for my younger self. I have since learned that self-care is a desire to nourish yourself, and it stems from self-love and includes unconditional forgiveness.

On top of all of my poor choices and desperate attempts to keep a man's attention, I didn't want to hurt anyone by completely cutting ties with them. I didn't want to repeat what had been done to me by someone

I wanted to care about me. I mean, what if they felt like I had abandoned them? I am cringing right now as I reflect on the truth in that question and how it caused me to stay curious long after the flame had burned out in a handful of relationships.

That is a season in my life for which I am thankful for and happy it has ended. Talk about toxic. It's uncomfortable to admit it, but this book is all about confessions, and I know I am not alone in this. My dysfunctional relationship with men started at a very young age. I know this for three reasons: one, I lived it; two, I'm a mental health counsellor; and three, I had a psychologist explain to me why I kept choosing the wrong guy. Praise the Lord, I've been healed. Through a slew of not-so-fabulous relationships, I eventually recognized my patterns. Yes, self-care includes looking in the mirror and taking responsibility for your behavior. I was behaving like a Fun Dip stick—you know, that candy that is two flavors of pure sugar and comes with a candy stick you lick and dip, but eventually you just eat it or throw it out and use your finger? Yes, that was how I was behaving. Sometimes I was the stick, and sometimes I was the sugar. If you're completely confused by what I am talking about, you might have to google what Fun Dip is or head to your local nostalgic candy store.

The greater realization I had, when I committed to healing and releasing my patterns, is that the dysfunctional relationship with men actually started with me and was caused by unprocessed pain. Reflecting on me, myself, and I allowed me to transform my relationship first with myself, second with what type of man I was available for, and third, it allowed me to attract an emotionally stable man who I have been married to for well over a decade and counting.

Every time you heal and release an old pattern, you transform your relationships.

A few months after losing a dear friend, my sister got married, and I moved out west to start a new chapter in my life. My teen years were difficult to navigate at times. They are for all of us, if we are honest about it. You get caught between wanting freedom, and uncertainty about who you are, and what you want to do with your life. I was eighteen, full of curiosity and ready for a dramatic change. I met a lot of awesome people and had a lot of fun in the mountains. In the process of being apart from my family, away from the only life I had known, I started to find myself.

Taking that leap of faith and hopping on that airplane afforded me the greatest opportunity of my life. I had to grow up—fast! I was alone, learning how to manage money for the first time in my life, and I was deep in regret because my mother and aunt had convinced me to cut my hair from waist length to a frizzed-out bob. It was worse than the mushroom cut. There are limited pictures from that season in my life because, well, frizzy hair.

I discovered a lot about who I was and what I was capable of while living in the mountains. I took more responsibility for myself, and I started to implement more boundaries, all while experiencing freedom like never before. I found out what it felt like to be wanted, and it felt good. Well, at least, temporarily. I am an overthinker—always have been and always will be. I've accepted that about myself, and I am okay with it.

Getting dressed for work early one morning, it hit me! I caught a glimpse of myself in the mirror. I started to tear up. What was wrong with the dudes from back in the day? Why had they treated me so poorly? More importantly, why did I tolerate it and make it mean that I wasn't beautiful? I quickly wiped my eyes, put on some lip gloss, and vowed to never put my worth in the hands of a man again. I'd left those people behind for a reason. I wanted to be far away from people who thought they knew me or judged me by things I had done. *No looking back* became my mantra. I was ready to let my past go, and that's exactly what I did.

There were a lot of fish in the sea for a young woman like me. Or should I say, bears in the mountains? Is that funny or nah? I made fast friends with people from all over North America—people who, like me, had hopped on airplanes and were keen on change. We all had one thing in common: we had all moved to the Canadian Rockies on a mission to find freedom. I was in awe! You wouldn't believe the people I met and connected with. Between my newfound friendships, crazy and fun coworkers, and all of the cool tourists I connected with, it was incredible. A reassurance from God that when you get that intuitive hit to take a risk and adventure into the unknown, you've got to go for it!

Let the good times roll. That was my motto. Seems superficial, but after years of being teased and feeling left out, it felt so good to fit in, to be wanted, and all of that happened by being myself. Alas, sooner than later, I inevitably had to say au revoir. I fell in love.

Looking back, I couldn't even imagine having stayed in my little hometown. Seriously, I cannot imagine it. I would not have blossomed into the real me, the woman I am today. I would have struggled to break free from the expectations placed upon me. I would have been consumed by the inner ache that penetrates deep in your bones when you prevent yourself from exploring possibilities. I believe everything I've gone through and accomplished has been preparation for the woman I am today. I am super grateful for every lesson on this ride of life. They have taught me a lot about myself and the significance of trusting myself.

When you embrace your uniqueness, *everything* changes. To be clear, I am grateful I grew up country. I am country at heart and always will be. There is a lot about my hometown that I respect, and I go back every once in a while, and I will be buried there. The plot has been bought.

Those stomping grounds are my roots, but I wasn't destined to stay there forever.

I have deep compassion for my former self that allowed guys to be so mean to me. How dare anyone try to make someone else feel less than. I now know it's a reflection of others' insecurities, but back then, I thought it was all my fault. I thought I was the ugly duckling who nobody would ever like. It's difficult at times to recall how I used to engage in such dysfunctional relationships before I learned how to love and accept myself. Before I prioritized my health and my desires. Keep reading; this story changes for the better. I have forgiven myself for acting out at times. I'm sure there are people who innocently got the brunt of my hurt. I have cut ties with that pain and refuse to identify with those years of my life. In addition to learning how to embrace who I am and love myself as I am, I also recognize the power in self-esteem and a positive attitude. There is nothing healthy about lingering in expired relationships, with friends or past lovers. Like Elsa said in the movie *Frozen*, "Let it go."

I had just turned thirty-five when it happened. A completely different example of letting go. I lost a parent. When my dad passed away—a slow, gut-wrenching process—I had to learn how to say goodbye and move on, believing his spirit is always with me. I had to create a new type of relationship with my dad. I'm still figuring out what that looks like because grief is a forever thing. Just when you think you've got it sorted out, pow! A new feeling emerges that you must face. A memory pops up, or you smell a familiar cologne or hear a certain song. Wham! Instant tears! Like a punch to the gut, it hits you hard.

There are connections and relationships that mean more than others, of course, and saying goodbye when you need to is liberating. It is also a self-care practice you need to develop and practice. Walking away from relationships that have served their purpose is not as complicated as some of us can make it. You know what I'm talking about here, right? We prolong the inevitable. We allow worry to take over our minds. We entertain thoughts that prevent us from taking action. Then, inevitably, the relationship in question will run its course, and we are left wondering why we waited. We question why we didn't tune into that inner voice earlier.

It is far more complicated to navigate all of the what-ifs while what you really want is out.

I had to learn two things: one, it is absolutely okay and healthy to outgrow relationships; and two, it is not necessary to linger in them when they've reached their expiration date. Some relationships have expiry dates we ignore, and then they end with dramatic chaos that was totally avoidable. Some relationships are forced to end by physical separation, like death. Then you have to figure out how you want to establish a different sort of relationship with that loved one. Every relationship that ends requires that you process your feelings. Too many people jump from relationship to relationship because they fear being alone; as a result of that, they do not gift themselves the power in self-exploration and healing. What happens is they take their emotional baggage with them everywhere they go and then wonder why patterns repeat themselves. Do you know someone like that? Are you that someone? What relationship from your past are you still carrying with you? Are you ready to release its hold on you?

My personal issue was that I never wanted anyone to feel like I had abandoned them. Sounds weird, but it's how I lived for a long time—ultimately, until I met my husband. When I met him, I knew I'd won the jackpot! He is so dreamy and artistic. His brown eyes melt my heart, and I love how he carries himself. He fell fast in love with me, and I, with hesitation, fell in love with him. I only hesitated because I grew up hearing if it looks too good to be true, it is.

There is zero doubt in my mind that God sent him to me. I had written my checklist of my dream man, and God delivered. He has been such a blessing in my life. He treats me like his queen and pours so much love into my life. He calls me his goddess and honors me and my body as such. We both have learned what true love is by being open and free to be who we truly are, together. That's what unconditional, safe, and stable love is all about. He has been a teacher for me in so many ways.

He is everything I had imagined in a partner. He has been, in an odd sense, a caregiver to me in ways that I never had growing up. He is so emotionally mature and patient with me and understands me on a level I've never been understood in my whole life. He has held sacred space for me and allowed me to be me. I have been able to open up and share all of the parts of me I hid and never shared with anyone before him. In turn, he has opened up his soul to me and shared pieces of his own life and past. We are in sync in a way I've never known before. Things are easy with him, not chaotic. As I looked up from my laptop, a blue jay flew by. Confirmation. God, I thank you. Whenever a blue jay flies by, I know it's my grandmother, my dad's mother, saying hello.

Where was I? Oh yeah. I was talking about the dramatic difference between clinging to a relationship out of fear and releasing it for someone even better. My husband and I came into each other's lives at the right moment. Divine timing. Although, to be honest, the first year was interesting. We had both experienced undesirable relationships. We were both healing in our own ways. Together we have evolved in such a beautiful and powerful way. We are so connected. It is incredible. I have never known love like this, and it keeps getting better and better. We host a weekly show on social media, every Wednesday, called The PRIMETIME HUMP Day Show, so we can help others couples create healthier marriages too. We have learned a lot over the sixteen years of our relationship, and we inspire our community by sharing strategies and solutions that help keep marriages strong, healthy, and fun!

I recognized that holding on to old relationships was actually hurting me and my current relationships. I accepted that the abandonment I had felt so deeply for so many years was not something I wanted to carry around with me anymore. I needed to release all empty relationships with confidence, trusting that I deserved to be loved honestly and deeply.

It started with the decision to fully embrace, accept, and love myself in the way I wanted to feel loved. My husband's unconditional love has helped me heal on levels he will never fully understand. He doesn't have to. Thankfully, prior to meeting my husband, I was entrenched in self-discovery and spiritual growth. My commitment to doing the inner work over the years is how I attracted my husband. I had a checklist, like I mentioned above. He fit the criteria, and I was ready for a man like that, and God did not disappoint. I have since developed a better understanding of the whole "people come into your life for a reason, season, lifetime" idea. It's a real thing. I do not take his love for granted, and I continue to work on myself in order to be the exceptional wife I desire to be. Part of building this kind of marriage is loving yourself so deeply and so unconditionally. I value my inner transformation and understand that I attracted him because of who I am—worthy and deserving. When you love and respect yourself, you are open to receiving that same kind of love from someone else. You cannot love someone else if you don't first love yourself. I see how innocently and easily it became my normal to hang on to people even when their purpose in my life had expired, but I also live freely now and have released the responsibility that belongs to others. Can you say emotional freedom? Perhaps you can relate. Maybe you have experienced this next level love for yourself, too. When is the last time you took inventory of the relationships in your life?

I highly recommend you do so, as soon as possible. I wrote about this in my book *PRIMETIME Success* and shared a valuable exercise for sorting through your inner circle in chapter 2. It's both enlightening and powerful. Hanging on to relationships for fear of being alone or not finding anyone better blocks your blessings. Assess and act accordingly.

Self-reflection is an empowering tool.

Here are some fantastic questions to journal on:

Do you accept yourself as you are?

Do you love yourself?

Who are you hanging on to that no longer serves a purpose in your life?

Why are you afraid to let them go?

Part of my self-care journey has been a mixture of healing myself and discovering what I need to feel my best. I now ask myself questions like that frequently. Attachment is human nature. We are attached to many people and things in a variety of ways for various reasons during different seasons of our lives, yes? For me personally, and perhaps for some of you, attachment to people or things is really all about our inner pain, wounds, traumas, fears, and sense of responsibility. Attachment to someone or something creates a connection, a bond of sorts. That doesn't mean it is a healthy connection by any stretch, but it is a connection nonetheless until you release it and let it go.

Through healing my own emotional pain, I learned that being overly attached to anything is not love. In fact, love is free, open, trusting, safe, while attachment and dependency are none of those things.

How do you maneuver through your relationships and friendships?

Have you ever continued to do things for somebody who betrayed you? Or what about the person who only reaches out when they need you or want to borrow money? How about the person who manipulated you, and when you finally had the courage and determination to exit the relationship, they poured on the charm, and along with all that sweetness, t(he)y guilted you into staying?

I believe we are all responsible for our own decisions, and I also believe that nobody can make us feel a certain way; however, it is truer than true that we are influenced by others and especially those we love or have a relationship with. This gets even more complicated when there is a sexual relationship involved. Hands up if you know what I'm talking about!

It's bad enough at times with a strictly platonic relationship. Mix in some sex and complicated emotions, and boom chakalaka. You've got an emotional mess.

Here is a poem I wrote long after ending a relationship with someone I didn't want to break up with but knew I had to—for my own sake, because, well ... self-respect.

All of those countless nights—
away with you, waiting up for you,
and wasted wondering
about ....
you.
All of those countless nights, gone.
Done. Lost. Memories.
Yet, still, I am up, at night,

wondering—where are you and

Most importantly, why didn't you care when I did?

I'm tired now.

When I sent you that message -it was because that's what a good woman is "supposed" to do—

Now I regret hitting send.

It was what it was and that's all that it was.

You—get out of my mind.

You look like poetry to me. Your eyes were like a familiar love song on repeat.

I, never realized how much I didn't need you,

Until you were inaccessible.

What I'm saying is ….

Au revoir.

Sidenote: Did you know that every single person you've ever had sex with has exchanged their energy with you, not just their bodily fluids? Interesting, eh?

While I'm all about women empowerment and advocacy, I'm also all about awareness and education. Be mindful of who you're exchanging energy with in every relationship, sexual or otherwise.

When you get intentional about your time, your energy, and your circle of influence and develop self-respect, you think differently about people and situations than you used to. It's one of the best gifts you'll ever give yourself, and it will create such inner peace that you won't be willing to lose it for the sake of a relationship. The right relationships—you know, the healthy ones—won't require you to choose between inner peace and chaos.

That saying *you never miss a good thing until its gone* is not always true. Believe that. Do yourself a favor and re-evaluate your relationships with an open mind and intentionally ask for guidance. Close your eyes, hand on your heart, and ask, "God, show me who needs to stay in my life and who needs to go." Pay attention to what comes up for you. Sometimes this exercise allows women to discover that indeed there are some unfulfilling and unhealthy relationships in their life. It's almost as if getting intentional about who you share your time and energy with gives you permission to be more selective. Grant yourself that permission and never look back. You deserve to be loved unconditionally, and that must start with yourself.

A Prayer for Guidance

Dear God, I know there are relationships in my life that need work—first with myself and my relationship to you but also with others. Please help me discern which relationships are healthy and which relationships no longer serve a purpose in my life. Thank you for the many blessings and amazing people in my life. I am ready to create healthy boundaries in my relationships and desire to be the best version of me. Amen.

CHAPTER 4

Confession: Supermarket Flowers Changed My Life

If you have ever put your face in a bouquet of sweet-smelling roses, you understand how powerful and beautiful the experience is. It's an overwhelming sensation of greatness. Positive sensory stimulation at its finest. It activates your joy factor almost instantaneously.

I treat my spiritual practice in the same way that I seek out beautiful flowers to enjoy, to get a sniff of, and to look at. The more I stop to inhale the great wonders of the world, the better I feel. The better I feel, the better I feel, and so it is. As it is with building your spiritual muscle. The more you trust the unknown, the more faith you create. The more faith you create—in both yourself and God, Source, the Universe, Creator, whatever resonates with you—the more you step out of your comfort zone and actually start living with less worry and more trust in all that is possible. Building your spiritual muscle leads to creating a safer environment for you to truly thrive in, through both mental and physical shifts. When you are connected to source energy, you will receive more clarity, trust your own wisdom, and feel more energetically aligned with the work you do. The more you focus on a faith-based life and believing things are working out in your favor, the less stress you'll experience. Your adrenal glands will thank you. Trust me on that one!

Here's the deal. You can give your energy to trusting in the unknown and focusing on the positive blessings in your life and step into a feeling of endless abundance, or you can feed your ego fears. Which feels better?

Think of a situation in your life where you felt overwhelmed and anxious with fears and worries that never even happened. Seriously, sister! Think about how many wasted sleepless nights, time spent overanalyzing emails, and empty conversations you have given your energy to and reflect on how many of your worst-case scenarios ever occurred. When you have programmed your mind to go to negative thoughts versus positive thoughts, it will happen on autopilot. That's how most of you have been living. It does not have to be that way. You can consciously choose a better thought in any moment. The more you start looking for positive thoughts and solutions, the more your mind will automatically start operating that way. What about all the space your unfounded fears took up in your head? If you're like me, at times it caused you to be snappy with your children or your partner, to overeat, or maybe it caused you to withdraw and isolate yourself from everybody, getting lost in your own thoughts and not showing up fully in your relationships and career.

How many of you are so familiar with fear and unconsciously comfortable with it because it's been your go-to preprogrammed pattern since you were a little girl? It is so familiar that the idea of trusting in the possibility of things going well for you and working out in your favor (also known as living in faith) seems like an unpredictable and unsafe concept and actually scarier than what you know—worry, anxious thoughts, and fear. It's the power of thoughts at work. You get to choose where you put your attention and energy.

Did you know that a *belief* is a thought you consistently think over and over and over again? Yes? Great news! You can choose to control your thoughts every minute of every day. You can stop the old thoughts and insert new thoughts immediately, so long as you are consciously aware of what you are actually thinking.

You can choose to think positive thoughts and trust that things will work out for you rather than engaging in the darkness of worry. Sure, it takes consistent practice, but it is totally life-changing. You get to decide: live life as you are or work to make it even better.

I have been teaching clients and audiences at conferences all about the power in our thoughts for years. I also wrote about the power in choosing powerful and positive thoughts in *PRIMETIME Success*, and the feedback from my readers was insanely good. We no longer have to carry our parents', or grandparents', or teachers' thoughts with us wherever we go. We get to choose healthier thoughts and change our narrative. It is possible. I am living proof of that, and you can be too. Some of you may be wondering if it's possible for you at this point in your life. Yes! It's not only possible, it is potentially the best thing you will ever do for yourself. Learning how to think differently takes time and focus, but it gets to be fun. Think of it as a self-love challenge. You start to become aware of your thoughts and how they feel in your body, and you pay attention to what thoughts feel good and what thoughts feel heavy or produce a nervous energy. One easy trick is to reframe the anxious feeling to excitement. Have you ever noticed that the racing heart and butterflies in your tummy are the same feelings you have when you are super excited about something as when you label the feeling anxiety?

Tune into your body sensations. Actually, feel the difference when you start functioning from a place of faith and ease and figure out how to maintain it for yourself.

Smelling beautiful, fresh flowers is like a *come to Jesus* moment for me every time because it allows me to pause, to fill my senses with a beautiful, soft scent, and to appreciate the magic in a rose, or any flower for that matter. I started buying myself flowers on weekly basis when getting groceries for my family many years ago. I remember the first time. I had a cart full of frozen goods and produce, and I'd walked past the flower section. I think I had gone back to the produce section to grab some lemons. Who knows! As I scoured the fresh flowers, I decided I was going to buy myself a bouquet to celebrate me. In that moment, I had a breakthrough. Why had I believed for so long that only men buy women flowers? What have I been missing out on? I proceeded to the checkout line, and the cashier asked, "Who are these beautiful flowers for?" I smiled and said proudly, "Me!" Insert the biggest eye roll here because that was her response. I prayed for her, hoping that she, too, would one day stop to smell the flowers and buy herself some just because! Research has proven that plants and flowers improve the oxygen in your home and up level your environment. Remember, what you surround yourself with is as important as who. Giving up your fear to God is ultimately your way of freeing up space in your heart and in your mind, which allows you to be fully present in your environment and relationships. It does not mean you will never feel fearful or experience things that feel overwhelming; it means you have an opportunity to connect with a higher power—an opportunity to release the pain, the fear, and the unnecessary worry and give it away. You cannot live a healthy life full of fear and anxiety. You just can't.

There is a better way. Will you take action?

Too many women fill their senses with painful thoughts, cluttered homes, crazy to-do lists, insane pressure to be perfect, overloaded calendars, and other things that lead down the path of overwhelming sensations, pesky doubts, racing thoughts, and fear-based energy. It sucks! Literally! It sucks the life right out of you. No more allowing fearful thoughts to push you around. Say it with me: "No more!" That's such an unhealthy way to exist, ladies! Living that way will completely drain you and take you to a place of constant mental struggle. It will also take years off your life, and leave you spiritually broken. Constantly operating in a stressed-out state isn't only harmful to your heart and adrenal glands; it affects every organ in your body. Choosing to shift your thoughts and consciously be mindful of what you are telling yourself and being influenced by will create more inner peace and harmony in your life. You deserve to live that life. You really do. Do you believe that? Do you understand the power in connecting with God? Do you acknowledge the opportunity staring you in the face to choose a better way of life?

When we learn how to pause and disrupt the autopilot pattern that we have been accustomed to functioning on and living in for so long, we learn how to become more present—mindful of where we are and what we are feeling. We also learn how to shed our ego in those experiences because we can detach from the busyness and tune into the here and now, and we are able to be in the moment instead of worrying about the next move. We get to stop and embrace the experience with no added pressure to be anything other than ourselves. Being in the moment and refraining from engaging in the mental chatter we so often fight off in our heads is cathartic. Start giving your attention to the beauty that surrounds you. If you find your environment cluttered or chaotic, do something about it.

We need to stop living in autopilot mode and start to embrace the here and now. We must shed the pressure to be someone we are not and start to truly tap into our soul desires, the woman we were born to be. We can only do that once we learn how to slow down and listen to our intuition, our inner voice, and connect with ourselves so deeply and divinely. When we tune into our heart and allow source energy to fill our body, we experience life in a totally new way. That action strips away the old self, what we used to identify with, and allows us to appreciate who we are now in this moment. There's no way you are the same woman you were two years ago, five years ago, or over a decade ago. It is simply not possible. Life events impact you, children grow up, marriages shift, relationships come and go, and you evolve through all of it.

Wouldn't if feel amazing to know and trust you don't have to do it all on your own anymore? Isn't it spectacular to understand you were created to live a bigger life and God is right here waiting for you to talk to him and ask for help?

If you haven't tried this, please don't wait any longer. You will begin to vibrate higher and step into the real you. Creating a faith-based life changes you at your core, forever.

The best tip I can give is to stop making excuses about why you can't access source energy, pray, meditate, or journal and start doing it. Five minutes a day. That's only a few minutes per day committed to your spiritual growth. Contrary to what some people say, there is no right or wrong way to pray, journal, or meditate. I actually use exercise as a meditative experience for me. Some people lie down in a dark room, others sit cross-legged on a yoga mat chanting om, some take off their shoes and ground themselves in nature. It's whatever works for you. I'm passionate about this because I grew up in organized religion where I constantly felt like I had to do things a certain way to receive God's approval and support. No! That's a lie straight from the devil. There is no right or wrong way for you to connect with spirit. It's a personal relationship, and it gets to be your own. No approval needed—only an open and willing heart.

You have to find what works for you and just do it. As a self-proclaimed prayer warrior, I'm constantly in prayer. I give thanks, and I pray for my life, my health, my intentions to be pure, and my thoughts to be positive, especially in challenging times. I pray for my husband and my son, other loved ones, my clients and colleagues, strangers on the internet, for God to take my troubles and to help me find solutions, you name it, I've prayed about it. Journaling is my go-to every morning. I sit in gratitude, enjoy fresh coffee, and write. Sometimes I ask myself questions, and other times I just put pen to paper and see what comes out. These experiences are different for all of us, and that's fantastic. There is no one-size-fits-all here. You get to decide what feels aligned for you, and then your job is to do it.

When it comes to the choices you are making, this chapter asks you to be more mindful and tuned into your thoughts and environment. Instead of defaulting to former habits, consciously choose to think and act differently.

Some of you have a spiritual muscle; it just needs to be reactivated. Perhaps you have experienced loss or great pain, which caused you to be angry at God. I have been there, sis! It's okay. Commit to living better. Commit to releasing the old stories and past experiences where you feel God let you down, and choose to trust again that you got through that, so you'll get through this.

One of my second greatest tips is to become a reflection of what you desire.

If you want more truth in your life, be more truthful.

If you want healthier relationships, stop gossiping.

If you want more love, be more loving.

If you crave more respect, give more respect.

If you want more faith, give more trust to God.

Build that spiritual muscle and watch your life fall into place.

Whenever you feel overwhelmed, whenever you feel scared or uncertain of what to do next, give it to God. Inner peace looks good on you, and that is the greatest gift you can give to yourself.

Remember who you are and buy yourself some flowers.

A Prayer for Guidance

Dear God, I've been struggling to feel connected to you. I want to trust in you. I want to feel better. I don't know what you need from me, but I am open and willing to connect with you in a new way. I believe there is hope for me, and I need to turn to faith more than ever now. I've been scared, and worry has consumed me. Please show me how to live differently. Amen.

POWER THOUGHTS FOR YOUR
SPIRITUAL GROWTH

I am connected to my source.

I am deeply loved and protected by source energy.

I am surrounded by love and light.

I am a powerful co-creator in my life.

I am inspiring others through my faith.

I am learning more and more about my innate spiritual gifts.

I am grateful to God for the blessings in my life.

I am abundantly blessed.

I am provided for at all times.

I am so deeply loved.

I am love.

I am free to be me.

I am speaking my truth.

I am open to receiving guidance.

I am willing to release old thoughts and believe new ones.

I am open to new possibilities.

MENTAL WELLNESS SELF-CARE

CHAPTER 5

Confession: I Stopped Making Carbs the Enemy

OMG, Becky, did she really just say that? Yeah, Sheila, I did.

Okay! Okay! I can feel you rolling your eyes at me. I mean, holistic health is all about green juice and chickpeas, right? Wrong!

Disclaimer: I am not a doctor, nor do I want to be, but I have witnessed thousands of people completely heal their lives by addressing their gut health. Mental health is directly linked to oral and digestive health. Don't believe me. Google it or ask your dentist.

It may be significant to also mention that I actually enjoy making my own green juice. Eating chickpeas …well, unless it's in premade hummus or bean salad, not so much!

For all intents and purposes, I'm confessing my forgiveness to carbohydrates because my dysfunctional love/hate relationship with them messed with my head and hurt my body in so many ways. What is it about the "c" word that has women feeling guilty or shameful? Why have we allowed society's influence and the atrocious diet culture, the multibillion-dollar industry that brainwashes us into thinking we are like pigs on the loose if we don't control every morsel of carbs that enter our mouths, convince us that carbs are the enemy? Why are we vilifying carbohydrates? Enlighten me, sis. Net carb, fiber count, simple carb, or complex carb;

where you at? I get a headache just thinking about having to track my macros and micros and all the other things I do in a day. I have a life to live, and too great of focus on calories and tracking led me to a distorted relationship with food and with myself.

At twenty-seven, I was crouched over on the couch. I hadn't eaten for hours because I was on a strict low-carb diet. I felt nauseous, irritable, and shaky and had actual abdominal pain. I couldn't eat anything yet because in my mind I had another hour of exercise to do before I could reward myself with food. I had drunk so much water that I was overhydrated. I remember that feeling because I could barely move. My son was asking, "Mommy, what's wrong?" and I was scared. *WTF am I doing to myself?* Yes, I was super thin, but my word, I was slowly slipping more and more away from who I was and who I was trying to be. Carb-free diets do not work for me. When I was creating my skinniest body, I obsessively tracked my caloric intake and freaked out if anyone interrupted me as I carefully entered my food and portion sizes while waiting to see if I had a good day or a bad one. My heart hurts a little admitting that. Even the mere thought of those days can cause me to feel sad and disappointed in myself. That obsession nearly killed me. Thankfully, through a complete lifestyle overhaul, and a lot of personal development, I am in a such a healthier place now and have been for years. Polar opposite way of living. I eat what I want when I want, guilt-free. The wound is pretty much closed, so it is safe for me to go there with you now.

I have profound compassion for those of you still stuck in the tracking cycle.

To live life as if God wants us to suffer and have unhealthy relationships with our body and food is insane. It's precisely why mental health issues and eating disorders go hand in hand. Not eating enough causes a lot of different things—anxiety, depression, and insomnia, to name a few. As does forgoing the nachos every single time you crave them, in my opinion. Any form of self-punishment or deprivation is unhealthy. What about the immediate sense of failure and shame we feel when indulging in too many cheese and crackers? Or even better, my personal favorite, a bag of dill pickle Doritos fresh out of the freezer? Do you put your chips in the freezer before eating them? Mmmm. Try it! Tag me on social with your fresh-out-of-the-freezer chips, and I'll definitely clap for you. It makes the experience so much better. If chips aren't your thing, cool! The point here is this: you are not worthy or unworthy based on the food you consume. Your worth is not in the bottom of a bag of chips, a loaf of bread, or any form of laxative. It's also not in a scale, tape measure, or the latest calorie counter app.

We all know that higher-vibrational foods like vegetables are so much better for us than chips, but honestly, unless you are eating chips every day and night, you'll be okay.

Now, reign it in. Let's not get too crazy up in here.

I am sharing this with you because I have always been an emotional eater and thought that was my destiny until I realized that change is possible. If I have struggled with this, I know some of you have too. We get so good at eating our feelings because it's socially acceptable. Far more acceptable than drinking them. We learn at a young age to swallow our feelings in one way or another because nice girls put other people's feelings first. Nice girls are skinny and pretty and popular. At whatever cost. Nice girls don't eat the last piece of pizza at the party or the crust; it's an unspoken rule.

Let's take a stroll down memory lane, shall we? Perhaps, you can relate to this.

When I was growing up, food was everywhere and was a go-to for all things.

Company was coming—fancy dinner.

Thanksgiving at my grandparents' farm—way too much food. Cheese platters for days.

I won at a spelling bee tournament—out for ice cream, triple scoop.

I was lonely and/or bored; it was nothing peanut butter toast couldn't solve. Or pizza, pizza-flavored crackers, or as an adult, wine, Doritos, pizza sub, or … Getting my point? (I love pizza and I love red wine). Zero apologies.

I am a work in progress, but I have come such a long way and feel so good about myself and my body. Although I have done a ton of inner work, I still catch myself at times feeling bad about what I have shoveled into my mouth. I am not a betting woman, but if I were, I'd bet that some of you are doing this to yourself too. Shaming yourself for eating a certain food group and then working out too long or restricting calories for too long. Then, lo and behold, you start the cycle up again.

It's the oh-so-familiar cycle of shaming yourself, guilting yourself, and wallowing in more emotional pain—over food! We deserve to live free of this mental anguish that we have created. Instead of blaming society, and marketing and diet culture specifically, I want you to fess up about your own struggles, your own cycle, and get help. There is a different way of life waiting for you, and society, marketing, and diet culture are not changing enough to help you. It's a personal journey, and only you hold the key. Sorting this relationship out is vital. It's not a relationship you can cut loose and wish well as you move on. You need to eat. You don't, however, have to feel alone as you sort it out.

I've got you, sister! We will overcome the emotional eating stuff together. We will not allow those unhealthy habits to rule our world any longer, right? We will eat what we want and not feel guilty about it. We will eat clean most of the time and therefore not go into a dizzy when we consume simple carbs. Can I get a witness? Thank you! *Now, if only it was that easy*, you're thinking. Well, what if it is?

I feel so strongly about this chapter because I was always the kid who got bullied for being fat. Until I lost seventy pounds in less than six months after having my son by diet alone. There were many years of weight/size battles. I actually cannot believe I succumbed to other people's perceptions of me for so long, because that would never happen now. I own my sexy. Sexy is not a size. It's a feeling. A vibe. A mood.

You may be wondering how I lost that kind of weight in that period of time. I took better care of myself and got intentional about what foods I ate, and more specifically, I became a conscious consumer. I will admit, I was hooked on a fat burner, too. Until, I made the decision to stop hurting myself and to start eating in a way that demonstrated how much I respected myself (even though at that time the respect was low). Slowly, I started feeling so proud of myself and my food choices, and the results I was experiencing were magical.

Everything changed. I was feeling more energetic. I was buying much smaller clothes. I was getting a lot more attention from men—and hot men! Not the average guy but the hot dude. I was getting some model gigs, did a commercial, and maintained my weight loss for about six years until I got really obsessed!

Releasing a lot of weight was supposed to make me feel better, right? I developed an unhealthy obsession and brutal relationship with my own self. The clinical term is body dysmorphia.

The irony here is my weight went from one extreme to another, and people *still* had opinions about it. I went from being too big to too skinny. Like birds chirping early in the morning, so too were the mouths of those around me.

My relationship with food was teeter-tottering on sickness, and my obsession with weighing myself was literally controlling my existence. I mean, I would step on the scale first thing in the morning, then after my morning water, then after my coffee, and again midday just to check on how the foods I had consumed affected my weight, and yes, then again before bed. I'm not proud of those years, truly. However, I no longer carry any shame around that unhealthy behavior. Hence, why I know which carbs (simple carbs, to be clear) I can eat without going over the edge into a full-on binge fest. I had to allow myself to eat simple carbs at times when I wanted to, because restricting them was leading me to yet another obsessive pattern. You see, as soon as I told myself I couldn't eat something, I started to crave it. Can you relate? It's like self-torture. I am not available to torture myself.

I'd avoid certain foods, as if a particular food group was the plague, all the while thinking about it, and boom! Hello, binge. So yes, my self-care includes eating whatever I want in moderation. The good news is, because I allow myself to eat what I want, I no longer obsess over foods, nor do I actually want to eat the junk foods very often. I tune into my hunger. Is it emotional or physical? Then I ask myself why I want to eat whatever it is, and if it's an emotional reason, like feeling sad or angry, I step away from the pantry. If it is because I actually want to indulge in a few handfuls of chips, or some hint of lime Tostitos with salsa, or what have you, then I go for it. Done and done. Are there any foods you know trigger you into unhealthy eating or affect you emotionally? Where can you start being more intentional and mindful in respect to your health and diet? What food behavior pattern are you currently in? Maybe you are free from emotional eating all together, and for that, I applaud you. That is incredible. For those of us who aren't, there is hope. Do not give up!

Part of me is asking myself WTF am I doing right now, getting so vulnerable, but if I've been through it, it's to help someone reading this going through it. I became very thin and very unhealthy. Yes! Emphasize the *very thin*, so thin that I lost all the parts of me I liked. Ahem! My boobs! I'm not kidding here. They literally shriveled up and, well, left me with some interesting changes, along with more stretch marks and some loose skin. Nice, eh? I'm bringing sexy back. Sexy is a vibe, ladies. It's not a size. It's not in smooth skin, and it's not lost in loose skin. I'm now in awe of my body and realize all persons have cellulite, stretch marks, and moles in weird places, and guess what? It has absolutely nothing to do with our beauty or worth. Do not, I repeat, do not allow your relationship with your body or with food to ruin your life. God has much better plans for you, gorgeous!

Here's some truth served up with a side of dirty fries. I was taking fat burners, restricting my diet—think extremely low carb and calorie restriction—throughout the day, and then at night … I was binging on candy, chips, chocolate bars, chocolate chips, whatever I could get my hands on. At one point, I was secretly hitting up several different drive-thrus and ordering everything from Tim Horton's cookies to Burger King onion rings. My entire day was consumed with what I wasn't going to eat, and then I ended each night with an explosive binge. I was full of shame. I was so angry that I couldn't control what I put into my mouth. I didn't trust myself, and I was exhausted. That period of my life was very disturbing, daunting, and nearly caused my death. *Not kidding.* I can't even imagine going back to that way of life because I've done so much inner work on myself and continue to. I truly see how beautiful I am and how incredible my body is now. My worth is not about what I do and don't eat. I am worthy because I am. Food does not dictate my value in this world. I do.

I live in such a different energetic state now. My confidence comes from loving myself inside out. I am no longer available to shame myself based on whether or not I consume a particular food group. I am no longer available to beat the shit out of my body, all while deteriorating my mental health. I am not a better woman if I don't eat carbs. I am a better woman when I take care of myself and when I am kind to myself.

It was scary to decide I was going to share pieces of my disordered eating journey with the world. I mean, I am supposed to have my stuff together all the time, aren't I?

For the record, the only reason I can safely write about this is because I am no longer triggered by the unhealthy patterns or topic. I've done the inner healing work for years, and I am here to inspire you to believe that it is possible to live free of self-sabotage and self-loathing thoughts and behavior and to say goodbye to disordered eating.

My past does not define me or make me less of a woman, and neither does yours. Can I get another witness?

I'm speaking to you right now, the woman who has battled this monster and the woman who is battling this monster right now. You will be okay. Get yourself the help you need. *Now.* Do not pass go. You are so deserving of freedom from this painful, lonely darkness. It's time to stop harassing yourself about what you eat and deciding whether or not you are worthy based on the food you consume. Your desperate attempt at controlling your impulses and weight are leading you to spend all of your energy thinking about food. You cannot get this time back.

There's more to the story of how unhealthy I became chasing after the thin life. I developed extremely low blood sugar, so fiercely low that after a brief hospitalization, I had to take my blood and test it four times per day for months. I literally had that yellow sharps container thingy. It was pretty bad, you guys, and you know what? Everyone around me, except for my husband, told me how amazing I looked. No one knew! Not a single soul. I was in one of the darkest periods of my life, yet on the outside things looked great. I felt so much shame. I was living out of integrity. I hadn't even disclosed to my partner how deep I was in the pit of self-loathing and binge disorder. I knew he knew something was going on but I couldn't bear to tell him the full truth of what my daily restrictions and binges actually were. I felt so embarrassed. I am a strong resilient powerhouse woman; how could he have ever trusted me if he knew what kind of lie I was living? I did eventually tell him. I had to. He was above and beyond confused, but empathetic. He was also scared.

You cannot be cruel to your body and be in alignment. It's not possible. Living in secrecy and shame affects every single relationship and experience.

I nearly had my driver's license taken from me. My driver's license, people! It was a dark and lonely time for me. Even writing this on paper in a book that is meant to help women, I feel a bit sketched out with myself for sharing, but I'm not going to minimize the truth of what disordered eating and body image issues do to women. I'm also not going to dim the light of possibility for all of you who know this fight or know someone fighting this. This can happen to anyone. It doesn't discriminate. There is light at the end of the tunnel. There is freedom from food obsession and body image issues. That is why I chose to share these pieces of my journey. Halleluiah!

I am a well-educated and extremely smart woman. If this impacted my life, it can impact anyone's. It does not mean you are dumb, weird, or mentally unstable. It means you have learned how to live with a disordered relationship to food and are in need of self-love and support to overcome it. It is frightening when I think back to how much control this unhealthy relationship had over me. I was embarrassed to ask for help because I was afraid of being judged. I worried that I'd never break free from that bullshit. I had created quite the web around myself, and it all began inside my head.

I will tell you with a smile on my face as I type this that I overcame those dark days. Through a lot of inner work and a commitment to health, I have put that (no longer a) secret and painful chapter of my life behind me. I can honestly say that it's been nearly a decade since I abused my body like that. If you are going through that kind of self-destruction and personal hell, please reach out to someone. I hid this secret from my husband for years, until one night after a binge I nearly dropped dead. Yes, it was that dramatic. I'd restricted my calories all day, had done two hours of exercise, had gone to work, and was so out of it by the time I pulled my car into the garage, he took me to the hospital. It's the secrecy that creates the shame. Believe that.

The doctor I met that night saved my life in more ways than he will ever know. In fact, I'll never get to tell him because that doctor later took his own life a few years later. I digress.

Self-care solution: I now eat simple carbs when and if I want to. I refuse to feel guilty about it. Actually, to be very clear, I refuse to fit into a box created by hungry women with a penchant for approval. I will not define myself by what I eat. I recognize the power in eating high-vibe foods. I allow my intuition to guide my eating. I focus on how certain foods make me feel. Sometimes I crave Tostitos, so I enjoy a handful or two. It's been very effective for me and takes away the relentless guilt and shame I used to feel. I am aware that too many make me feel bloated, irritable, and just not my sexy self! I know my limits, and honoring them is self-care in and of itself. I refuse to label food good or bad. I have learned that labels like that create an energetic vibration of the food or drink we consume. I know it sounds crazy to those of you who are not tuned into the concept of frequency and vibration, but it is true. Think of it next time you eat a food you deem bad, and see how it affects you and your thoughts. You cannot eat a food you've labeled as bad and feel good. It's not possible.

Quick solution: remove the labels you have placed on foods and eat what you want in moderation or according to your dietary needs.

I have much more control than I used to and can consciously say no when I choose to, but restricting any particular food group from my diet in the name of self-care backfired on me in a very horrific and dangerous way, and it could be affecting you too. I refuse to allow any food category to dictate my sense of worth, and I encourage you to do the same.

Self-care includes loving your body as you are and wanting to be healthier from a place of love, not punishment. You deserve to enjoy your food.

A Prayer for Guidance

Dear God, I am in such an unhealthy place right now with how I feed and treat my body. I am ready to love myself more and free myself from this warped relationship I have created with food. Please help me find the right support and proper care team to work with me as I overcome these inner emotional demons. I need your guidance and forgiveness. Please help me forgive myself and to love myself as I am. Amen.

CHAPTER 6

Confession: I Unplugged from the Buzz

Do you remember the days when we used to talk to one another face-to-face? I'm starting this chapter off like an old love song from the nineties because, well, it's appropriate. You know, when you actually sat face-to-face and made eye contact while you talked to a real person? Never having to wonder who you were speaking to because they were live in living color. No profile pic or meme, a real person. What about the good old days, before cell phones were invented, when we picked up the phone and dialed the number to call a friend? Some of you will recall the rotary phone (I dreaded the numbers that were all nines), and some of you may only recall the push buttons. Either way, do you remember having to use the phone to communicate voice to voice, and if the person you were trying to reach wasn't home, it either rang one hundred times or went to an old, outdated message on an answering machine, which was saved on a tiny little cassette tape, back in the days before automated voice mail existed?

What about the dreaded busy signal? Beep, beep, beep. If you got the busy signal, you'd pace around, excessively hitting redial, or you would run down the street to your friend's house because obviously some chatterbox was holding up the line. You could get to their house before their older sister hung up.

Yes, it's true. There were limited options back in the day, yet we survived. My parents didn't invest in call waiting for many years long after it was available, and same goes for the long cord. They didn't see the point. It was pretty much an open conversation for anyone in the house to eavesdrop on during any phone call because the curly and always knotted phone cords didn't stretch too far from home base. Now, we text and DM whoever we want to, and nobody knows what we're saying or sending except for the person on the other end. What about those encrypted, secret, dissolving messages Messenger allows you to send now so you don't get caught cheating—I mean, so nobody can access your secret messages?

My parents only bought the extended cord after wires kept popping through the original because it was constantly being stretched to its limit. If your parents were like mine and didn't want to fork out the extra dough for any fancy features, you pretty much fought your sister for the phone on a daily basis. I laugh, but explaining these truths to my nineteen-year-old son is next level. He's a smart dude, yet all he knows is life with technology, and I'm grateful for it. I'm pretty tech savvy myself; I've had to learn the ins and outs for many reasons, like parental responsibilities, running a location-independent business, and being able to check my money. My son assists me when needed. It's usually something so simple like needing to update my settings, but still, it's great to have the extra help.

Why my husband and I talk to him about days gone by is because it helps him understand us better and why we feel so strongly that FaceTime (although I love it) is not the same as in-person communication. Times are changing, and we can choose to get in the know or struggle to function with modern-day technology. Besides, who doesn't appreciate a great Snapchat filter?

There's something even bigger here though. Our attachment to our handy-dandy smartphones is affecting our brain chemistry. Research articles I've read over the years consistently outline symptoms like headaches, vision problems, neck pain, sleeplessness, irritability, and even depression as potential risk factors. Several clients have reported an increase in their anxiety with excessive scrolling and screen time. Which, as a woman running an online business is not avoidable but it is controllable. I researched the impact of screen time and social media on concussions after my son had his third one, and let me tell you, it was mind-blowing. Google it for yourself or even search the impact of screen time on the human mind and read through some scholarly articles. It is fascinating to learn how a tool we rely on every day for communicative purposes and entertainment is putting us at risk for things most people wouldn't imagine.

I had to set an example. I had to cut the cord. I unplugged from the internet and the apps and shut off my notifications. No, not forever but for periods of time. I do this as part of my self-care.

I have committed to less screen time and more face time. Part of caring for yourself is taking action on the knowledge you obtain, not just sitting on it, so to speak. Knowledge is not powerful; taking action is.

After choosing to be more mindful of when I use my phone and how I use it, I immediately experienced these benefits: less squinting, more focus, less FOMO (fear of missing out), and better relationships. There are two major rules in our household: one, no phones at the dinner table; and two, no phones in your bedroom. Now that my son is a young adult, that one has shifted. When he was younger and up until eighteen years old, his phone was charging in the sitting area, not his bedroom. I made sure of it! I was the phone police, for reals! Those were the years of abundant eye rolls!

Too many people wake up after a restless night of half-ass sleep because their phone has been buzzing and dinging throughout the night, and they immediately get on their phone. My first thought is, *Why in tarnation are you sleeping with your phone?* And my second thought is, *No wonder you feel like crap*. It's become an epidemic, hasn't it? Groggy, fried brains as a result of smartphone addiction. Hands up if you, too, have been guilty of this. For some people, especially those who live alone, their only source of connection with family, friends, and strangers on the internet is through social media, email and apps. My personal favorite is Instagram.

My wish is that you take care of yourself like you do your phone— actually, even better, care for yourselves. That's relatable, isn't it? All jokes aside?

I mean, nowadays, we all have a smartphone or know someone who does. The phone consumes most of our time and mental space. We are super conscious of which color of phone we buy and the type of case we keep it safe in. We pay extra for the military-grade screen protector, we purchase a screen cleaner, we invest in device protection, and on and on. We go into debt sometimes for a piece of technology that most of us are convinced we can't live without.

We know where it is at all times, and we have more than enough chargers so that we are never stuck with a dead battery. We create secret apps to hide our secrets. Oh, and let's not leave out the fact that we have so many emotional moments with our phones. We use it for texting, photoshoots, messaging through various apps, and of course to get social on whatever media apps we just can't live without.

So, how about putting that type of time and energy into yourself? What a concept, eh? Can you even imagine how your life would change if you invested in yourself as much as you do that phone you carry around with you?

Would you select an otter box for your body's protection or a cheap dollar store case? Would you invest in great skin care or slop on the cheapest shea butter product? I'm being oh so serious! For reals, girl! Would you think twice about putting the same kind of money and time into yourself as you do your phone? What about upgrading your mindset like you update your Instagram app?

I know who I am, and the journey to becoming my best self has taught me and continues to teach me how important self-care, in all the ways, in all the things, really is. The interesting thing is this: the term *self-care* is used all the time, and it gets lame really fast. I don't think you have to use that term religiously to benefit from the results. That's what this entire book is going to demonstrate.

I also believe that living our best life includes consistent evolution. It is not a one-and-done type adventure.

I love my phone. I do. It allows me to connect with family, friends, and clients all over the world at any given time. During the COVID-19 pandemic, when I was editing this book two years after writing it, I used my phone every single day to communicate with my family and clients. I was in Florida for months, alone, and my family was home in Canada. Trust me when I say I love my phone and technology in general. It has opened up many opportunities for me and my business. I have my favorite social media apps, and yes, I love the Fitbit tracker. What I don't love is the fact that people expect instant replies, instant likes, and all the other crap they've come to expect because, of course, everyone is always on their phone. Nope! Not today! Put the phone down, turn off your read receipts, and be present with your partner, your children, your friends. Sit and actually hold a conversation at dinner instead of scrolling mindlessly. Watch your relationships improve simply because you are focused and not distracted. The greatest reward of unplugging has been the time I've gained. I encourage you to track how much time you are on your phone for one week—heck, one day. Include checking emails, texting, playing games, swiping left or right on Tinder, scrolling Instagram and Facebook, and any other activities you use your phone for. Then tally up how much time that is taking away from your life. What else could you be doing with those hours? Where could you be putting your time and energy? An easy way to measure your screen time is in your phone settings. You can receive weekly updates on how much you're using your phone. Every week that my screen time goes down, I celebrate!

One of the greatest challenges many people face is the FOMO (fear of missing out). They think that their celebrity crush or the lady boss they're secretly stalking on social will post something and they'll miss it. Calm down, sis! It's an app. Don't let it control you and your attitude. You aren't missing out on anything except inner peace. I have actually unfollowed a lot of people over the last few months. I grew bored of their presets or overly polished feed. I don't compare my life to others on the internet, but I do want to follow people who inspire me, light me up, and whose feed makes me feel high vibe. I want to follow and connect with real people, not a projected fake image. I hope you evaluate who you're following too. It's a great self-care tip! Sometimes you may not even realize how the energy of who you follow and consume content from is impacting you until you click unfollow. I created a wonderful meditation series called the PRIMETIME Detox Kit that has eight audio tracks, and the entire purpose of that series is to teach you how to unclutter your mind and life, to empower yourself to be mindful and aware in all moments. One of the best things I've ever done is go through a digital detox. Go on a digital diet and see how you feel. You can always refollow if you must. Own your time and take back your power over the apps that have you feigning for more. Jokes aside, technology—our phones specifically—are becoming an addiction.

Here are a few other useful tips to help you unplug:

- Set boundaries around screen time.
- Download a self-care app tracker.
- Turn your phone off at night.
- Involve an accountability partner.

There's a lot to be said about how our hunched-over hand-holding screen time is causing neck pain, poor posture, and carpel tunnel. Just say no and prioritize your health.

A Prayer for Guidance

Dear God, I have been consuming way too much media and relying on my phone for communication. I need a break. Please help me recognize the value in face-to-face conversation and allow me to better manage my time spent on my phone. I am ready and willing to let go of my instant gratification issues and live free of social media obsession. Amen.

CHAPTER 7

Confession: I Stopped Negotiating with Myself

I stopped talking myself out of doing what I knew I had to do. Negotiating with yourself can be dangerous. It's a sabotaging tactic that will keep you stuck and stop you from changing. I always say that stuck is a decision, not a destination. Negotiating business contracts, payment plans on a new vehicle, credit card interest payments, or things like that are not the same as the contracts you have with yourself. When you gain clarity on who you want to be and how you want to live, you have to safeguard those decisions and act accordingly. What this looked like for me could be similar to what it looks like for you.

I stopped making justifications for why people were treating me a certain way, and I took ownership of my decisions to communicate with them and responsibility for the necessary boundaries I needed to implement. I decided I was no longer available to accommodate other people's needs at the sacrifice of my own.

The negotiations you have with yourself determine the quality of your health and your relationships. There will be opportunities for growth and negotiation within your mind as you commit to changes, of course, but I'm talking about the potential of negotiating yourself into a toxic situation, or out of a personal commitment you've made like going to the gym, or eating less sugar, or maintaining a regular sleep schedule. If negotiating with yourself leads to prosperous opportunities and results, fabulous, but if it derails you and prevents you from becoming your best self, it's a problem.

I read something spectacular in the *Harvard Business Review* written by Erica Fox that highlighted this exact topic. She wrote about four key players that we all have on our inner negotiator team:

1. The Dreamer
2. The Thinker
3. The Lover
4. The Warrior

These guys help shape you into who you are and govern how you behave. In summing up what she wrote, we learn that the Dreamer is all about intuition. The Thinker is all about logic and reason. The Lover is all about emotions, and the Warrior is all about action. Pretty fascinating, eh? Instead of asking yourself which one best describes you, the better question is to ask yourself, how are you showing up, and what skills are you using moment to moment?

Take a minute right now and ask yourself, How are you functioning in your current situation? Are you fueled by emotion, taking action toward your goal, overthinking an argument with your partner, or visualizing your big dream? What's your vibe like? Are you feeling good or are you feeling drained, frustrated, or disrespected?

The more you tune into what you're thinking and what you're feeling, the more effective you'll be at creating the life you desire. Positive negotiations only happen when you are feeling positive—and vice versa. Make sense?

One popular attitude buzzing on the internet that I want to explore is the craze of memes with the saying No F*cks Given written on them. While that may seem cool and super badass to many people, it feels way off the mark for me. You see, everything in my life changed when I actually started to give a f*ck.

Now, if you are easily offended by this word, like my sweet momma is, and don't want to read a chapter in a self-help book that uses a four-letter word like that, stay with me. Switch the word out for a different four-letter word that resonates with you. Example: I started to give more care, or I started to give more love, or whatever. You get the point.

When I stopped and thought about my life, the people in it who I care about, and the incredible impact I strive to have through my business and books, I recognized that giving zero f*cks was not beneficial for me. Nor was it the attitude I wanted to teach my son. Now, don't get me wrong; let's not get this twisted. I have a personal policy that states no one's opinion is my reality, and I do what I need to do for myself and my family at all times without feeling guilty. So, there's that. However, when it comes to living my best life, I now give more f*cks about my health, my mental wellness, my circle of influence, and my environment, and I give way more f*cks about the people who are important to me.

I remember how life used to be—you know, before I started being intentional with my time and focus. I had an attitude problem, and my self-talk was off the chain. Mostly, because I wasn't happy with choices I'd made in the past, I was annoyed with myself for letting the weight creep up on me without doing much about it, I was carrying shame about things that weren't mine to carry, I wasn't 100 percent happy with my business, I was still paying off mounds of debt, and of course, there were other issues that had lingered on too long, like the dysfunctional relationship with myself. It became obvious to me that the only person who could change any of this unhappiness was me. I'd let my attitude of "I don't give a crap" go on for too long. In case you are one of the rarest women on the face of the planet and have never struggled with an attitude problem, I'll give you some ideas of how that type of attitude affected me. I'd say I was committing to healthier eating, and then I'd crave a full plate of nachos, and because my husband craved them too, it was easy for me to say, "EFF it! I don't care about what I feel like," (knowing full well that consuming a plate or even a half plate of nachos would cause me to feel bloated and angry at myself for having zero willpower), and I'd gorge away. Or what about the millions of times I'd say, "I'll start tomorrow because YOLO!" Yup, proof of no f*cks given! There have been different occasions in my life where I did not make the best decisions for myself. When you are at war with your body, you tend to treat it poorly. When you walk around with a chip on your shoulder, you not only hurt yourself but others around you too. It's a completely low vibe and extremely unattractive.

It was my *I don't give a rip* attitude that caused a lot of problems in my life. Another way this can show up is through grudges. Are you the kind of woman who never lets go of a hurt? Do you walk around angry at your mother? Father? Sibling? Child? An ex? An employer or employee? If you are, you have to learn the power of forgiveness. It's not about anyone but you. Carrying that emotional turmoil is literally eating at you and taking years off of your life.

The attitude of not caring about anything is leading you down the path of eventually having to care about everything because it's like a tornado, and the aftermath is not pretty.

When you give zero f*cks about anything, everything falls apart.

As a result of figuring it out—you know, that I actually needed to give a f*ck about myself, my health, and how I am living—everything shifted for me. In doing so, I started to make way better decisions and choices about what I ate, how I thought, how I showed up for my loved ones and for my business, and most importantly, how I respected myself. Did you know that caring about yourself is demonstrated through thoughts, behavior, and your habits? It's clear to see when you look around you who cares about themselves and who doesn't. This isn't rocket science. Personally, I wish I could make every single one of you care so deeply about yourself that you commit to an up level like none other, but I know it is not my responsibility. Only you can make that decision. When I made it, *everything* changed for the better and continues to. I do mean everything. I became very intentional about my self-talk, my morning routine, my circle of influence, my relationship with my body, my commitment to feeling better—essentially, all of the things that self-care improves in our lives. You don't need a master's degree to know that taking care of yourself leads to you feeling better about yourself, and when you feel better about yourself, you live better and love better.

My identity changed when I no longer lived as the *I don't give a crap* kind of woman because my mind-set changed, and yours can too. Start paying attention to your inner dialogue and evaluate how often you are negotiating with yourself in a way that no longer serves you or who you want to be.

Ask yourself, What do you really care about? In other words, what matters to you? Who truly matters to you? Do they know how important they are in your life? How are you showing up for them? For your responsibilities?

You see, unless you start truly caring about the quality of your life, you will not be able to create the best of the best, and isn't that what we all desire? To feel good and live better? Yes?

I want to break it down for you in a way that makes even more sense.

If you go through life with a chip on your shoulder—not giving a f*ck about what anyone says, thinks, or does—cool, *but* if you go through life not caring about what you say, think, or do, *look out*! Danger, danger! That's a recipe for disaster.

A big piece of the self-care puzzle is taking care of your mind. Your mental wellness directly affects your health. How you talk to yourself matters so much that no wonder some of you feel like you're running on a hamster wheel. You need to get off it once and for all.

How? Start by intentionally speaking positive words to and about yourself. Start giving a f*ck about being kind to yourself. Start appreciating your health, your vision, your mobility, your family, your opportunities, your freedom. Yes, that sounds trite, but many of you have lost sight of those fundamental blessings and abilities.

When you go back to the basics and start truly honoring all that you are and all that you have, you'll quickly discover that the kindness you give to yourself allows you to give more kindness to others. Winning! You'll also recognize that many of the negative thoughts or words you use toward yourself are linked to past pain. You might be repeating putdowns from a parent or sibling. You may be reciting the words of a mean teacher or sports coach. You may be replaying the tape of a toxic ex whose voice still plays loudly in your mind. Check in with yourself and ask, "When did I start believing this?" and consciously choose to flip the script. It's time to heal old wounds, release past pain, and build a healthy relationship with yourself. You are never too old or too young to experience self-love and respect.

A change in attitude leads to a change in perspective and, essentially, a change in the stories you tell yourself about who you are and what is possible for you. A lot of the "I don't give a f*ck" attitude comes from people who have had their heart, spirit, and soul hurt by people who did not care for them in the way they needed or desired. I get it! As you read through this book, it is clear. Hello! I started prioritizing self-care because of all the pain and heartache in my life. So, ask yourself if you too have held on to the hurt for too long, and explore whether or not you need to adjust your attitude and start giving a f*ck.

When is the last time you took inventory on who you are, how you live, and what you do? I encourage you to do so regularly but especially now, before you move on to the next chapter.

Where in your life is it clear that you give a crap, versus where in your life is it clear that you don't? What are the stories you tell yourself about yourself?

Here are some common ones I hear from clients all the time:

- I grew up poor.
- It's in my genes to be overweight.
- I never have enough time.
- I don't have the energy to workout.
- My husband doesn't support me.
- My kids don't appreciate me.
- I'm not a morning person.
- I don't journal.
- My knees are bad.
- Therapy is for weak people.

Do any of those sound familiar to you? Can you relate?

If you don't care about your financial struggles, you will surely attract more.

If you don't care about your weight, you will surely gain more.

If you don't prioritize your time, you will surely struggle with finding any.

If you don't exercise, you will surely never have more energy.

If you don't communicate with your husband, you will surely feel like he doesn't support you.

If you don't talk to your kids about respecting you and your time, you will surely feel unappreciated.

If you keep telling yourself you're not a morning person, you will surely never get up earlier.

If you don't make an effort to journal, you will surely never be someone who journals.

If you don't believe in talking out your problems, then you will surely attract more problems.

When you start taking responsibility for your attitude, and only then, you start caring about how you feel and how you function in your everyday life. At the end of the day, it matters; you matter. You are a pretty big deal. Your life is in your hands. Checking your attitude gets to be fun, and it is necessary. The world doesn't owe you anything you refuse to work for, and neither do your relationships.

Changing your attitude to improve your life is priceless, and it's free! You don't have to pay a dime. I mean, you can. Hiring counselors and coaches is amazing and speeds up the process, but you don't have to. You can make a decision right here right now to focus on being a more positive and upbeat person. A person who looks at situations with the glass half-full, not half-empty. A person who doesn't linger in blame and finger pointing and takes responsibility for her life and her results. A person who no longer negotiates with herself about her goals or boundaries.

Will you commit to exploring your attitude?

Will you commit to caring more about yourself than you ever have?

For some of you, this concept may sound crazy. If you're like me, you were raised to believe that women take care of their men, and they cook, clean, raise the children, hold a job while they hold down the fort, and put everyone else's needs before their own. Oh my! If you have ever flown, you know without a doubt that you put your oxygen mask on first, not your child's and not your husband's, so why live the opposite way? It's okay to do all those things, by the way, *if* you want to. The whole point here is to get clear about how you want to live and then live that way.

Be who you want to be and live bolder, louder, larger than ever. Share your best self with the world, refuse to do things out of obligation, and choose to live on purpose.

A Prayer for Guidance

Dear God, I've been feeling resentful about all the commitments I have made to people. Sometimes I wish I had just said no. I am ready to change my attitude and transform my relationships, first with myself and second with everyone else. Please help me think more positive thoughts and to show up as the woman I desire to be. Amen.

CHAPTER 8

Confession: I Was Angry at God

In life, we experience so many different things: pain, happy times, death, birth, loss, challenges, and such. As a result of the highs and lows we experience, we create memories that are stored in our minds and impact how we show up in relationships. We also build resilience and enhance our capacity to grow, succeed, and maintain the lifestyle we desire. There's one extremely powerful self-care practice I have learned to indulge in, and that, my friends, is the power in a good snot-nosed cry. I, like many of you, have gone through many challenging times. This particular challenge I am going to share made me not only question my faith but grow angry at my source, my God. You know, we've all done dumb things at times, risky things, and we learn from them. I, for the most part, have been a very faithful servant. As a woman of faith, I have always turned to God for hope, guidance, and direction. There was this one time though that I wanted to turn away. I felt betrayed. I felt lost. I felt angry.

Two weeks after my twenty-first birthday, I became a mother. How interesting, life-changing, and amazing it was to experience pregnancy and carry such precious life inside of me and to be blessed with a beautiful bundle of joy. I mean, the privilege and honor of becoming a mother is something I have never and will never take for granted. I am so grateful that I was fortunate to experience such a miracle.

I'm writing this chapter at the cottage. It's been a family tradition for well over a decade now to head to a cottage near Algonquin Park in northern

Ontario, Canada, every summer. It's 7:50 a.m. I'm snuggled up in a blanket, sipping Folgers coffee with my laptop and looking out the big bay window that allows me to see through the trees all the way down to the water. Tears of love and joy fill my eyes so quickly as I watch my son fish off the dock. He loves to fish, always has, and hopefully, he always will. He casts with his left hand and reels the line in with his right, something the specialists said he would never do. I'm fascinated by him. He ignites a love in me I never imagined possible. The way he moves through life—energetic, funny, and always up for an adventure.

You'd never know his battles, unless you know. I know them all too well. That is his story to tell, if he ever chooses to. I have his permission to write about my experience on our mom and son journey.

The same day I became a mother, I also became an advocate, an investigator, and a terrified and confused woman. When most new mothers are trying to figure out which diaper is best and won't leak, I had an entire slew of research to do, medical terms to learn, and support services to schedule and sort out.

"There's something wrong with our son's arm," my husband said approximately twelve hours after we had been set up and moved into our semi-private room at the hospital.

"Huh? What are you talking about? He's been swaddled and bundled up cute as a button since I delivered him. He's absolutely perfect!"

"No, his arm, it's different than the other one."

I quickly unwrapped my son from his tightly swaddled blanket and examined his arms. "Oh my God! What is happening? Yes, there is a drastic difference in them," I cried.

"What is this? What's going on? What happened to him?"

"Nurse! Nurse! We need some help in here!"

My heart sank, and my thoughts started racing. I was still trying to process everything that had occurred during my son's delivery, and now there was another problem. I picked up my son and held him tight against my chest. I don't really know what was going through my mind at that moment, but it certainly was not at all related to what I was about to hear. I was frozen in time.

Everything happened so quickly. I was informed that my son had a rare physical condition called Erb's palsy and had experienced a brachial plexus injury during delivery.

Erb's palsy: paralysis affecting the muscles of the upper arm and shoulder that is caused by an injury during birth to the upper part of the brachial plexus. (*Merriam-Webster Dictionary*)

Brachial plexus: a network of nerves lying mostly in the armpit and supplying nerves to the chest, shoulder, and arm. (*Merriam-Webster Dictionary*)

I was in shock. I was speechless. I couldn't look at my husband; I stared at the wall, then looked back at my son, then back to the wall. As I looked down at my son's innocent face, tears streamed down my cheeks like never before. I had never cried so hard in my entire life. I was suddenly overwhelmed with a deep, gut-wrenching sadness that no mother should ever have to feel. All I could think was, *WTF? He has what now? Come again? What the heck is that? Will it heal? What does this mean? How will this impact my son? Why my son? Why me?*

As I lifted my gaze up to my husband's face, he looked at me with such an unforgettable expression. I remember it to this day. We were both scared.

In that moment, I started rerunning the tape of my labor in my mind. It was like a bad movie that I was desperately trying to rewind and pause. I will never forget that feeling sitting heavily on my chest and in the pit of my stomach. It was a pivotal experience that not only changed me but obviously shaped who I am as mother. That moment demanded a next-level version of my twenty-one-year-old self. There I was, a first-time mother who had gone through a traumatic delivery, and now I had learned that something was wrong with my baby. I didn't receive much information other than a referral to physiotherapy services and well wishes. As I lay back down in my hospital bed, tears of anger, fear, and confusion poured out of me. Why was this happening? I was furious with God in that moment. I hugged my son and whispered, "Together, we will get through this." I refused to accept the term *physically disabled* only because I didn't know enough about the conditions or the long-term effects. I knew two things for sure: one, I had a difficult journey of motherhood ahead of me; and two, my son would surpass any limitations spoken over him that day. I was going to make damn sure he did. That was certain. Nothing else was at that point.

I remember crying myself to sleep for many nights, all the while thinking, *God, what happened? Why my son? Why did you allow this to happen to my son? After all I have done to be a good Christian, why this?* I was so confused. I didn't want anyone to know because I didn't want other people's fears put into my head. What was I going to do? *My body has failed me! God, you have failed me! You have completely failed my son! How could you? Give me a miracle, Lord. Heal him. Help us figure this out. Do something! Anything!*

I was terrified, I was alone, and I had gone emotionally numb.

I remember feeling like I'd been throat punched by a five-hundred-pound boxing champion. I didn't know what to do. My body had been through the ringer, I didn't want visitors, and the picture-perfect opportunities I had envisioned of capturing our new family's joy didn't happen. I was so confused and in shock for many days. Needless to say, when I opened the flood gates, I could not close them. I cried for days. I remember holding my son close and praying for a miracle night after night. I prayed for knowledge, help, guidance, answers, and with a grateful heart, I thanked God for my son. I started to shift from feeling furious at God to being focused on facts. I had to. It was the beginning of a slippery slope into a dark shadow called post-partum depression. I knew I had to find a blessing; something other than my fear to focus on or else I would be in trouble. What if he had not survived the delivery? My mind was racing, and I had to sort it out because I now had a life to take care of. I declared in that moment that my son would not only use his arm, but he would live a life far greater than I had ever imagined for him. I vowed to not stop researching, advocating, and speaking health over my son until he experienced healing that would allow him to live whatever type of life he would want to live, doing whatever he would one day want to do. I refused to label him, and I refused to give up.

The specialists and support workers must have thought I was bat-shit crazy because although there were many worst-case scenarios, I chose to talk about only best-case scenarios. Do you know how difficult that was for me at that point in my life? Twenty-one, new mother, and not taking the doctors' speculation as facts. Mama bear came out to play, and I refused to let this slip under the radar. I chose not to take the disability forms they wanted to send me off with, and together, my son and I walked out of that hospital and headed for home. I was so desperate to start building my relationship with my son outside of the hospital setting. I wanted to take him home. I wanted to bond with my son away from the bright lights and call bells.

As we pulled into the garage, I experienced a deep sense of relief. I literally burst into tears of gratitude. I gently touched my son's face and said, "Welcome home!"

I am forever thankful to be my son's mother. It's been quite the journey from then to now. It's been gut-wrenching at times and a seemingly endless fight for answers. If new mothers are usually exhausted, I was a real-life mom-zombie. I lived on zero sleep for months. Those days, although not forgotten, rarely enter my mind now. When they do, it can bring me to my knees in heartache, still to this day. Although much healing has occurred and continues to, there is never a day that goes by that I don't pray for another miracle. I will never stop praying for more healing. I can't even tell you how many people fluff it off and say things like, "Well, he looks normal," or "He's okay." I get that they don't have the emotional connection, history, or concerns because they are not his mother, but saying things like that does not comfort; they piss me off and minimize my feelings, my reality, and my son's. However, I choose to focus on the blessings that have been given and stay true to my promise of never giving up. Self-care includes addressing the not-so-good stuff, but you don't have to stay in it. Expressing emotions does not mean living in them. Besides, I have witnessed miracles, and therefore, I believe more than ever that the big guy has bigger plans. My faith was completely gutted and overhauled through this experience. If you don't have hope in one thing, how can you have hope in anything?

There were times when I felt robbed of the normal new-mom moments. It's difficult to admit, but there were times when I just wanted everything to be normal. I wanted to live life with my new baby and without the medical and specialists' appointments. They were taxing on me, and mentally, I was tapped out. I was experiencing grief and fear when I thought it would be excitement and joy. Night after night, I experienced flashbacks and nightmares of my delivery. I had attended all of my prenatal classes and had not even thought about having a problematic birth. It has been extremely painful to relive those moments in such detail as I write this chapter, but I know there are other women out there who have experienced difficult deliveries and psychological scarring as a result. I want to be a voice for women who may feel like they don't have one or maybe aren't sure what to say. Health care providers need to be aware of the impact that traumatic births have on mental wellness. It's not limited to postpartum depression; there can also be PTSD symptoms that need treatment. Women, we need to educate ourselves and advocate for our health, not just for our children.

Allowing myself to sit in the feeling was my self-care. Instead of forcing myself to feel happy or grateful all the time, I allowed myself to cry, to feel sad, to embrace the mixture of emotions when they hit me. It was my therapy; it was how I managed to function and get through each day. I didn't put any expectations on how I was supposed to feel. I didn't pretend I was doing great; that would have been even more exhausting. I chose not to share information with people outside of my inner circle and therefore felt lonely much of the time. I was afraid that if too many people knew, they'd tell others and share the wrong information. I couldn't bear the thought of people labeling my son or gossiping behind our backs. Instead, I chose to trust and believe things would get better day by day as I did the assigned physio exercises and poured all my love into my son's healing. Thinking back, I realize how mentally tough I was. No one paused for a second to inquire about my well-being or my mental wellness. Postpartum checks weren't really a thing, and other than my six-week checkup with my OB gyn, there were no healthy-baby clinics to go to. Somewhere in all the chaos and what soon had become my new normal—medical appointments, checkups, specialists' appointments, and at-home physio exercises—I started to find much pleasure in being a mom. My son was the happiest little boy, always up for a snuggle and so easygoing (except for the colic he experienced for the first few months). Did you know that babies who endure traumatic deliveries tend to have colic? I learned that from one of the specialists I went to.

I love that boy with all my heart, and I will forever. The things we have been through together are mind-blowing, yet here we are! Nineteen years later and going strong. He is a real badass! His positive demeanor, his desire to do whatever he wants, and his commitment to living his best life are true examples of children living what they learn. Moving forward, accepting it is what it is, and appreciating the possibilities created a different vibe, a healthier energy, and ultimately, produced more miracles. As his mother, my instincts are on point. I know he struggles with challenges he faces. It hurts. I still cry a lot. Then I wipe my tears and thank God for possibilities.

Who knew that a snotty-nosed, deep sob could be so therapeutic? A gut-wrenching, painful, "I don't know what to do, but I'm waiting for a miracle" kind of sob. I opened the flood gates in order to not lose my sanity, to maintain emotional stability, and to be able to show up as Mom. Crying is an energetic release for me, and it was the only release I had. The bonus was I could do it in private—just me and my boxes of Kleenex. The first few years were very difficult. It's hard to know what's happening with a child who cannot tell you where it hurts or how they feel. There is nothing worse than feeling helpless as a mother. That's one of the reasons the tears flowed. It helped release all the thoughts and feelings associated with all the things being a mother of a child with different needs involves. Does that make sense? Have you ever experienced such grief and heartache about someone that you literally cannot find words to express your feelings, but the tears flow nonstop? That's what I'm talking about. I had a pastor who once told me tears are a language that only God understands. I believe that.

To fill in some of the blanks, I will tell you that learning how to be the best advocate for my son was a full-time job, but I did it, and it got better and better for me and him. I spent a great deal of time researching his diagnoses and seeking out holistic healers. I tried to find local support groups to go to, but the only support group I have ever found after all these years is a Facebook group based out of the UK. I didn't have anyone to ask about it because nobody, including the doctors I called, knew much or had anything to say. I had to use the computer at the library or my parents' house because I didn't have a computer, and smartphones didn't exist. If I ever felt alone, it was then, and I'm thankful to be where I'm at with it all now. Surviving the first three years of my son's life were a good mix between nerve-wracking, rewarding, and scary as hell. Throughout that time, my marriage fell apart. I was a single mother, broke, alone, and trying to do the best I could with what I had, which wasn't much of anything, except I had my son, and that was all I needed. He inspired me to keep going in my darkest days and to become the woman I am today.

His smiles and hugs were everything to me, and they still are. I am so passionate about teaching women how to release old pain stories, boost their confidence, and become financially fit as a result of everything I have grown through. Being spiritually fit allows women to be connected to a source far greater than themselves, which allows abundance in health, money, and relationships to pour into their lives. It changes the entire game for women and their children. Trust me when I say I learned that the hard way. I registered for college to earn my second diploma and worked as much as I could to pay the bills and provide the extra care my son required. Thankfully, although not excitedly, my parents let me move back in with them.

As grateful as I was at the time to be fortunate enough to have a roof over our heads, *nobody* wants to have to go back to their parents' house, no matter how cool their parents are, especially with a child in tow. It was about a year or so of reliving pieces of my childhood while being a mother—brutal. Some of the unsupportive people in my family who were looking in from the outside thought it was a free ride. No, it was definitely not free! It had a cost—a cost so steep those judgmental folks couldn't have paid it if they had to. Isn't it funny how family members can be the most unsupportive and judgmental people in our lives? I will always be grateful to my parents for stepping up and helping me in the ways that they could, but nobody will ever know how difficult that one and half years were for me. They were some of the most challenging days in my entire life and also some of the greatest character-building years. I am forever appreciative of the people who stood beside me and not behind me, casting judgments and gossiping about things they had no clue of. Moving along …

To be able to speak life over my son and watch him do things that the specialists and doctors said he would never do has given me a glimpse into what God is capable of; miracles happen every day. You need to believe it to see it! Whatever you are going through right now, choose to find the positives, the blessings, and focus on those things. Whatever you seek, you'll find.

One of the greatest blessings from all of this has been the fact that my painful, grief-stricken, and confusing journey as a mother has now become another woman's survival guide. There are so many women raising children with different abilities and characteristics and also feeling so lost and alone. Figuring out your groove as a mom is difficult enough. Add the extra responsibilities required, depending on your child's needs, and boom! It's even more challenging. Am I right or am I right?

I know without a shadow of doubt that God knew I could and would handle having a child with physical abilities associated with Erb's palsy and brachial plexus injuries. I'm a natural and resilient leader. It's in my DNA. I always figure things out, always.

This is the part where I tell you that my struggle is real.

It's never stopped; it's only gotten easier as my son has gotten older. Every single woman I know that has children, is pregnant, or wants to be pregnant has big, audacious dreams for her child.

I am no exception.

I carried a healthy baby boy to thirty-nine weeks before being induced.

The injuries and physical issues my son lives with happened at the time of birth. It was preventable, yet, clearly, it was destined to happen.

Through many sleepless nights and tears that I thought would never end, I learned how to forgive everyone involved. That's why I have moved on and not lingered in anger. I had to allow myself to grieve all of the unknowns and all of the milestones and moments my son would not be able to experience due to his injuries. That was a process, let me tell you. I also had to dig deep within my heart and soul and forgive God too.

The daily prayers, trusting God to heal my son through guiding me to the right doctors and specialists, were not always easy, but they were the only source of comfort I had then and still have. It's not easy nineteen years later, and it most likely never will be. I still have genuine fears and concerns about my son's progression and physical health. I still have moments of anger that this happened to my son, but I have come a long, long way. I had to allow myself to grieve and come to terms with what is my normal as a mother. I remember feeling so angry at God, for many things actually. Have you ever been angry at God? Surely, I am not alone here.

Here I was, divorced, a single mom, financially broken, and having to deal with all the responsibilities that most parents share. I was desperate but hopeful.

I had to rewire my mind and start thinking about the positive things that were going on, or I would've lost it. I had to accept that this had happened for a reason. My son was healthy throughout my entire pregnancy, and everything changed during delivery. Why? Why my son? Why me? I was *angry* until I wasn't anymore. Anger stems from fear and hurt, and giving all those crazy emotions and worries to God really helped. It allowed me to express my anger and clear my mind at the same time.

I'm an action taker; sitting idly in emotion doesn't work for me. The more I learned, the better I could advocate. I had to shift my perspective. My life literally depended on it, and at that time, so did my son's.

As I'm sure some of you understand, it's hard to be a healthy and present mother when you're full of anger. It only causes more issues and pain in your household.

My faith grew exponentially as a result of all the things I went through and continues to.

It's so interesting to me to watch my son in action—tying his ties, lacing up his work boots, writing, playing ball, fishing, and so on. He has figured out how to do so many things that blow my mind and the minds of his doctors. I mean, yes, I worked on his arm for years when he was a baby, toddler, and young child, but once he started being able to move it and use it, he surpassed any goals with a smile on his face! That little seven-pound baby has grown into a six-foot-two young man. He is such an incredible inspiration and source of love in my life. You might be wondering, How did he progress and heal? There's been a lot of physio and massage in his life. There is still a lot of healing for him to go through, and if you're a prayer warrior, please say one for him! He can use his arm with some limitations at this time and continues to experience miracles. He doesn't know anything different, so his journey has been a bit different, and I respect that. He's nowhere near regular; he's definitely PRIMETIME. I am so proud of him. I am so proud of *us*! As I mentioned earlier, there are still moments when things hit me hard, but all in all, I am so grateful for this journey, and I wouldn't have wanted to go through it with any other kid! It's all about perspective. I had to choose to find joy in some of the darkest and most challenging moments in my life. It was a minute-to-minute choice at times, and if you are struggling with something, anything, it is imperative that you choose to find something positive in the chaos while allowing yourself to feel your feelings. Shutting them off or shoving them down your throat only leads to more pain for you.

Life calls us to rise up, and God does not give us anything we cannot handle. Trust in that, and you will find that inner power to fight the good fight. I am rooting for you. You are not alone.

In awareness and honor of individuals living with Erb's palsy and brachial plexus injuries, raise a hand for those who can't and shout it from the rooftop that *anything* is possible when you choose faith over fear.

A Prayer for Guidance

Dear God, I am so angry with you right now. I don't understand why this has happened, and I am having a hard time pulling on my faith. I want to feel better. I want to forgive you. I trust you to heal this situation. I am ready to move past the anger and into emotional freedom. Please protect me and guide me so that I know what to do next. Amen.

POWER THOUGHTS FOR
MENTAL WELLNESS

I am worthy of love and happiness.

I am focused on improving my health.

I am feeding my mind with positivity.

I am surrounded by people who are healthy in mind, body, and spirit.

I am responsible for my mental health.

I eat to fuel my mind.

I am grateful for my body, and it shows.

I am kind in word, thought, and deed.

I am so happy and grateful that I am alive.

I move my body, and it soothes my mind.

I am blessed with abundant health.

I am focused and fabulous.

I am in control of my mood.

I choose to find the positive in all situations.

I have the power within me to create the life I desire.

I forgive myself and free myself from the past.

PHYSICAL WELL-BEING SELF-CARE

CHAPTER 9

Confession: I Was Raised by Well-Behaved Women

It's nine o'clock on a Friday night, and I'm ready to wind down and go to bed. I love my bed. I love my pillows, high-thread count linens, and duvet. And, of course, I love all the things I do in my bed—getting quality sleep and snuggling up to my lover. My bed is a safe haven for me, and getting adequate sleep is high on my priority list. In fact, it's non-negotiable. Everyone who knows me knows I'm an early riser. I haven't used an alarm clock for fifteen years, at least. I haven't needed to. My internal wake-up call comes anywhere between 6:00 and 6:15 a.m. Guaranteed. I had to figure out how much sleep I need to function at the level I desire to function at in everyday life because lying around in bed after enough sleep is not for me! Some people thoroughly enjoy just lying there, but unless I'm meditating upon waking, I've got to jump up and claim the greatness in the day ahead of me. I was raised by nighthawks. Both my mother and my grandmother were women who stayed up late—after the eleven o'clock news, at least. I'm completely the opposite. Nine-thirty is a great time to call it a day in my mind.

I was raised by tired women who followed all the rules and put everyone else before themselves. I grew up around women who loved their families so deeply and so proudly. It sounds wonderful, doesn't it? From my perspective, the price those women paid to be the diligent and submissive wives and the seen and unheard women within their own households was enough for me to recognize that there is no badge of honor in being well behaved.

To me, it seemed expensive. It caused tension in my body to think that my entire existence would revolve around other people. Add to that people who wouldn't necessarily appreciate me or my time. All mothers raise your hand because I know you can relate to that in some way.

It is neither right nor wrong; it just is what it is. I am very grateful for my upbringing. It taught me all about the ways in which I did not want to exist in this world or in a marriage, and it also allowed me to learn how to love unconditionally and to appreciate health and opportunities afforded to me. I am different. I am an eagle. I was born to soar. I was born to explore. I have opinions. Lots of them. I like to be seen and heard. I have very important things to say. It's time to shine. Where is the microphone?

I'm not like those women. I am extremely different in many ways from the women who raised me. Mostly, because I am not available to be seen and not heard. Been there, done that. I've got the bumper stickers, the T-shirt, and the scars. I am never going back to being invisible, no matter what it costs me. I am not a people-pleaser anymore, and I prioritize myself over others. I am not available for less than I desire, and I make no apologies for how I live. I love and respect the women who raised me, yet I know and have always known that God created me for such a different life. Such a time as this. A time when women everywhere are being given the opportunity to rise up, to lead, and to share their voice. I was never going to live the same way as those women did, and I have always been aware of that. I used to struggle with why I couldn't just be happy doing what they did. However, once I realized that being true to my values is what matters most, I released the struggle.

A woman who puts everybody else before herself cannot make magic happen. A well-behaved woman worries too much about being referred to as nice, and me, well, I'm in a league of my own. I have an extra-large personality, and there is nothing unladylike about it. I know there are women out there like me. Women who have a calling to change the way in which women show up in the world. Women who understand that being kind and thoughtful is a part of being a badass and equally understand that saying no is extremely important in all relationships. Women who don't apologize for being well educated, sexy, and ambitious. Women who don't put their husband's needs before their own. Women who understand that self-care isn't a luxury, it's a necessity. I know these women run rampant waving their hands high because I have had the privilege of working with them. Are you one of us? If yes, you are safe here. In fact, you are encouraged to embrace who you are in such a positive and loving way that nobody holds power over you and your choices. Women who speak up are welcome here. We have been created for such a time as this. Together we are changing the world for the better. Congratulations on owning your fierce factor. You fit in here simply by being true to who you are. Isn't that refreshing?

When you are different from all the other women in your family, you feel it. You know it. Sometimes you wonder if you're cut from the same cloth, and other times you relish in the differences. There comes a point when you figure out that the leading ladies in your life were examples for you growing up, and they were neither good nor bad; they were demonstrating contrasting lifestyles than what you want and need. As you mature, you learn to accept the differences and celebrate them. You recognize that having an opinion doesn't make you rude, inappropriate, or less of a lady. It means you're a woman with her own thoughts, and you don't shrink or play small in order to be liked. Empowered women can empower other women to step into who they were created to be without any shame or judgment.

I have always had an entirely different vision for my life than the women who raised me. I don't know exactly what they envisioned for me but I know it wasn't what I imagined. I have different ideas, desires, needs, and I've created a variety of opportunities to step into more of the woman I must become to have the lifestyle I want to have. I'm super grateful for the lessons learned along the journey to being myself. As a result of getting clear on who I am and what I need I have attracted incredible blessings into my life. Thank you! More please!

I have more freedom and abundant opportunities than both of my favorite women had, and I appreciate it. I live a different lifestyle, and that's absolutely okay. I go after what I want and do not allow anyone to talk me out of my dreams. I have built my confidence to this level because I trust myself and I trust God does not give any of us a vision for our lives that we cannot fulfill. Also, as much as it can be fun to play the submissive role at times, I am an alpha femme. I am not bossy, sis! I am the boss.

I have no issues with the fact that my husband dotes on me and vice versa. All great men know how to take care of their woman, even when she's an independent badass who can take care of herself. (I love being doted on by my king!) Not only do I love it, it's a requirement for me. I was clear about that prior to getting married, and let me tell you, when you attract your ideal partner, they will align with your requirements. Men want us to tell them how we need to be loved! True story! They are incredible partners when we communicate with clarity and assertiveness. Men dig that! Well, at least men who want to be the man their wife desires.

The more I embraced my differences, the more success I experienced. I have zero apologies for my lengthy and impressive education. I don't pretend to be un-opinionated either. Growing up, my parents never talked about post-secondary education. Mostly, because they could not afford to send me away to school but also because it wasn't a conversation in our home. There was no extra merit put into ongoing education for numerous reasons. So, as much as a lot of successful women haven't earned degrees and diplomas; I have and I am extremely proud of myself. I learned so much about myself and gained many transferrable skills throughout my years in post-secondary. I have no regrets about the insane amounts of time and money I have invested in my education. University teaches you a lot about the power in being different. Women do not need to diminish the hard work they have devoted toward stepping into their greatness in or outside of the classroom.

Please, ladies! Stop acting like you're okay with things you're not okay with and use the word *no* as a full sentence. It is safe for you to be a beautiful and smart woman. It is safe for you to be the real you. The woman who wants to be pampered, the woman who wants to experience the finer things in life, the woman who wants to drive a fancy car and not a minivan. Too many of you are showing up as the woman you think people want you to be, heck, that's why some of you did go to college. There is so much more to you than meets the eye. Pretending to be satisfied with anything less than your truth is sucking the life right out of you. There is no badge of honor in being loyal to others and not yourself. In fact, it's an expense that will cost you your inner peace.

Can you relate to feeling different from the women around you? Have you ever had a moment when you questioned how you fit into the family you were born into because they feel so unrelatable? What about your friendships that may have faded?

I choose to do all the things that my grandmother never had the opportunity to do. Whether she would have or not isn't the issue; it's the freedom of choice, and I don't take it for granted.

My goals and dreams are big, so big that they scare most people around me—and at times even myself. I heard that means I am on the right track. I continue to evolve as a woman and think bigger all the time. There is no limit to what I can do, except self-imposed limits.

I firmly believe that God created all of us to evolve as individuals and that it's our duty to use whatever is thrown at us for fuel to be better and to help others. The beauty is in the transformation, and so is the lesson.

I didn't stick around the small village I grew up in, and I didn't marry a guy I grew up with. As Garth Brooks said, "Sometimes I thank God for unanswered prayers!"

Many women have never left that small village, and that's totally cool. I loved growing up on my grandparents' farm. I am country through and through but I always knew that I would leave. At eighteen, I hopped on a plane and never looked back. I may have physically gone back years later, but the old me that everyone thought they knew never returned. She was gone. That version of me didn't exist anymore. I completely transformed myself, and that started the personal development journey and self-love journey I've been on ever since. I'm an adventurous soul. I take risks, and I have learned many lessons the hard way. Remember, I have opinions!

I was raised by women who did what they were told, and although some think that's what good girls do, I look at it as oppressive. I will not have "she was a good girl" on my tombstone when I die. More like "Badass mother who showed her son what was possible and created her best life by being unrealistic." Whoop there it is! I'm living while I'm alive and unafraid of what people think of me. I cared for way too long, and it literally ate at me because I never felt like I was good enough for anybody. The toll that took on my mental wellness, body, and soul was brutal.

God has blessed me with so many experiences that have led me to appreciate that being different is incredible. It hasn't always been so sparkly and fun. The path to self-acceptance has been more like a twister at times. Being true to who I am is the only healthy and sustainable way to live in integrity. I want you to experience the inner peace that comes with accepting yourself as you are and as you blossom into the woman you want to be. No running away from fear. No settling. No pretending to be satisfied with anything, and no apologies for being you. That's how you become confident in yourself. You stay true to yourself. When you embrace your badassery, you change your life.

Being a badass takes energy. A lot of energy. Positive energy at that. Hence, I like to be in bed early. I need my rest to recharge for the next day of living on purpose.

Being who you are is the secret ingredient in your recipe for success. Creating your life to fit your needs takes guts, especially in a world where women are constantly subjected to the media and marketing scandals that rely on making us feel like we aren't good enough as we are. If we buy their product, we will be better. If we wear more makeup, we will be beautiful. If we say yes to things and people we don't want to say yes to, we are nice girls. If we struggle with losing the last five pounds, we are more relatable. Ugh! As if! No way, José! That sounds like a slow and painful death to me. Life is for the living! It's PRIMETIME to *shine*, and, gorgeous, it's time to stop dimming your light.

Let me put this into perspective, how many of you have women in your family who didn't have the right to vote, let alone pursue an education? What about women who were shipped off to live in a school for difficult and rebellious girls? Doesn't that make you want to own your voice and shout to the world who you are and get on with living the life you desire on your terms, not waiting for permission or approval from anyone? It makes me want to scream at the top of my lungs that women have been seen and not heard long enough, and it's time to step up and into our fierce feminine power without worry of not being good enough, or too much for others. I, personally, am like guacamole. I am extra AF and I am okay with that. Women who love themselves live differently. They recognize the value in caring for their own needs first because it allows them to be a healthier, more present partner, mother, lover, business owner, and employee. Healthy women make better decisions and make more money.

There is no badge of honor for the woman who puts everyone before herself. There is, however, a thing called burnout waiting for her. That's no way to exist.

Women who forfeit sleep or exercise to be at the beck and call of another are not living their best life. They cannot. They're exhausted and most likely filling up with resentment. When is the last time you said no to someone you love without justifying it or explaining why? In my book *EXPOSED: Diary of a Self-Care Junkie*, I shared a poem that got women fired up. It goes like this: "Stop feeling like you have to justify yourself to everyone. No means no, in and outside of the bedroom." What do you feel when you say no to someone? Do you feel like you let them down, or do you feel empowered? Stop saying yes when you mean no, and let your no be no without any explanations. It will change your life, sis!

Growing up, my grandmother was very involved in our church, as was my mother. I volunteered and ran junior church for a while and enjoyed it, but there came a point when things were expected of me and my time. It was not a *hell yes* by any stretch, yet I did those things out of sheer obligation. No more. I refuse to do something because someone wants me to or because it is expected of me. I won't do it for two reasons: one, it is not aligned spiritual behavior to be doing something out of obligation; it feels gross. Two, it's not my responsibility to be all the things to all the people. It may come as a surprise to some of you, but I used to do all sorts of things I didn't want to do in order to fit in and be liked. Still, it got me nowhere. The cost of living that way is insecurities, anger, and poor self-esteem. I have grown as a woman in many areas of my life, and the best tip I can give you about building self-respect and confidence is respecting your no's. Do not allow yourself to operate from a place of desperation to fit in. It will cost you way too much and leave you empty.

I have been blessed with a husband who supports me in all things and admires my no-bullshit approach to life. I am so grateful to have a man in my life who encourages me to be exactly who I desire to be. He realized a long time ago that a happy wife equals a happy life, and he reaps the benefits in many ways. All jokes aside, don't get it twisted. Being an empowered and conscious woman means I encourage my husband to be the best version of himself, too. I love sharing our dreams and desires and then holding each other accountable to do all the things. Marriage is a partnership. We are so connected on a such a deep level that we can seriously read each other's minds. It's kind of creepy and kind of cool. We have been sharing content weekly for years via our PRIMETIME HUMP Day Show every Wednesday because we want people like you to have a next level marriage too. Go to my Facebook page to check out the videos. They get thousands of views, and it truly lights us up. We created the show to help spread more love and loyalty in the world. Monogamy is not dead, FYI.

How are you showing up in your marriage? Your friendships? Your business or career? Are you energized and confident, or are you depleted and frustrated? Are you repeating patterns you learned while growing up, watching the women in your life?

At times in my life, I have had to physically remove myself from situations. I hopped on an airplane at eighteen, never having flown before, and moved out west. I didn't know anyone where I was going, but I had to get out of dodge. I had to do something with my life, and I knew I had to take a risk on me. Later on, I had to physically leave a marriage. That was hard. Looking back, I understand why it had to happen, but hindsight is always twenty-twenty. The hard relationships and lessons in life aren't always understood until a later time. I share these examples to inspire you that whatever situation you are in right now that feels daunting or frustrating, there is a better way. Maybe you need to have a tough conversation with someone. Maybe you need to leave a relationship that no longer meets your needs or has become toxic. Maybe you have become toxic because you spend all of your time trying to live up to other people's standards or expectations. Whatever it is, trust that you will get through it and come out the other side wiser and better than before.

Taking responsibility for our lives includes having to do things we don't always want to do but know we need to. Asserting your voice in a new way can be scary, but what's worse is never changing and never living life the way you want to out of fear of being shamed or judged for being different. You are not a freak because you are different from the other women in your family. You're allowed to be your own version of a powerhouse woman. You can be different and still love and respect the women who raised you. It is safe for you to be seen and to be heard, gorgeous. Your time is now. Get your badass beauty rest. You're going to need it.

A Prayer for Guidance

Dear God, I need your direction right now. I feel so out of place within my family at times, and it's uncomfortable. I want to learn how to fully honor the woman you created me to be. I want to tap into my intuition and value my uniqueness. Please help me to show up as the woman you desire me to be and allow me to be a positive influence in the relationships I value. Thank you for creating me to be different. I am ready to embrace the real me. Amen.

CHAPTER 10

Confession: I Stopped Chasing the Perfect Body

I have a penchant for workout clothes. I love bright and funky capri-style leggings and top-of-the-line sports bras, and I enjoy having all the cool sayings splashed across my tanks. I literally get up each morning and throw on my workout gear. That's my routine. It has been for years. It ensures my morning workout gets done. No excuses. Until recently, I had been chasing my perfect body. One workout at a time. I was certain I'd find it. I thought having a fancy gym membership and awesome workout clothes would help me sweat my way to it. For nearly two years, I spent a lot of money on a fancy gym membership. I worked out five days a week doing grueling yet transformative exercises that ended up leaving me both sore and feeling accomplished, on the daily. I justified it with the fact that spending that kind of money each year (almost $3,500) proved I was invested in improving my health, releasing weight, and tightening up my body. Didn't it? I mean, a lot of people couldn't afford that kind of fitness program, but I could. That is, until I couldn't.

Injury after injury was proving to be the sign that I in fact needed to give up my fancy-pants gym membership. I was hiding behind it. I was in the "working for my perfect body" club, but my hamstrings were screaming at me every morning when I got out of bed. That's what women do who are struggling with body image issues. We pop fish oils capsules, mix a pre-workout drink, do our workout, but don't prioritize stretching, and then we drink wine in the afternoon, or was that just me? The search for my perfect body had to end. I didn't know where she was, but it wasn't in the gym.

I had to cut the shit and get real with myself. My perfect body was the body I was living in.

It's really easy for me to look around a gym and spot the women with body dysmorphia. I've been there. I can pinpoint the behavior immediately. It used to trigger me. It caused me to workout in ways that were hurting my body, not helping it. I mean, the personal trainers are right. You cannot out train a bad diet. Believe me, I have tried several times. It does not work.

I had to explore new exercise options that aligned with my abilities and did not increase or cause further injury. I was going to see my physiotherapist almost weekly for those two years. I mean, what was I thinking? It wasn't really about that though either.

I was at a physio appointment one day when it hit me. Why on earth was I continuing to spend money at a gym doing a program that wasn't working for me? Duh! What was I chasing?

It was about an hour after that when I contacted the gym and said I wouldn't be back. My renewal was about to kick in, and it was the perfect time to get out. I was getting creative with my at-home workouts. I have a home gym, and Google allows access to thousands of free workouts. I decided that exercise needed to bring me joy; otherwise, I wouldn't do it.

I had contemplated water aerobics for a while because I knew exercising in the water was far easier on your joints and therapeutic in and of itself. Let's face it, I had let my weight creep up to a number that didn't allow me to do heavy jumping and weight bearing activities; it hurt my little ankles. I digress. However, was that what old ladies did? Could I really release extra weight doing aqua-fit or was it solely social hour? No offense to any of my new aqua friends, I love you dearly, but originally, I didn't think it was an exercise for a woman in her thirties.

I bought a membership at a local YMCA, specifically for the aqua fitness programs. I can say, exercising in your swimsuit definitely builds body confidence! I went at least three times a week and would aim for five. The irony here is the money I was spending on that fancy-pants membership now goes toward swimsuits! Huzzah. Word to the woman contemplating this form of exercise – you need to support your ladies, if you know what I mean. Spend the money on a quality swimsuit, it is worth it. You'll be bouncing around and you don't want anyone losing an eye.

Some of you might be in a position right now that you can't afford any type of gym membership. No worries, the world is your playground. Your body is your vehicle. You can move it any way you like, so long as you move it. Why we complicate the whole exercise thing is beyond me. Every time I move my body I feel good, and yet, my inside voice is screaming "flatter abs, tighter butt, leaner legs, c'mon push harder, don't stop!" As a result of all the mindset work and healing I have done I now scream back NO! I will not over-do it and I will not treat my body with disrespect. I stop when I need to. I want you to remember that your physical body that stares back at you in the mirror is transporting you around. It is not you. You are not your body. Got it?

There are so many things you can do to get your body moving, all while having fun.

Here are some free ideas for you:

- ✓ Decide you're the type of woman who exercises daily.
- ✓ Go for a walk.
- ✓ Do a hundred jumping jacks at lunchtime.
- ✓ Stretch in the morning when you get up.
- ✓ Borrow a yoga or exercise DVD from your library and do it at home.
- ✓ Grab two cans of soup to use as weights and do arm movements.
- ✓ Bicycle legs during TV commercials.
- ✓ Crank up your favorite tune and dance.
- ✓ Google free exercise videos on YouTube.
- ✓ Park a far distance away from the store and get more steps in.
- ✓ Get up from your desk often and jog on the spot.

Whatever you do, stop making excuses about why you can't work out.

Every time you choose not to move your body, you're telling yourself you don't matter. Our bodies were designed to move. When you choose to feed your excuses and not your desire to feel better, you will continue to struggle.

Don't get it twisted; it's not about looking a certain way. Exercising is imperative to not only your physical health but your mental health as well, and the more often you get up and move your body, the more energy you will start to have, and the better quality of sleep you will start experiencing. Did you know that your manifesting powers are activated through movement too? Get up and shake your booty, sis!

I remember thinking that exercise was a form of punishment or a way to burn a certain number of calories so that I could indulge in bread or wine or whatever food it was at the time that I was restricting. Maybe some of you are still thinking that way. It's not a positive mindset, but even more than that, it's not a healthy way to live. We get to move our bodies because we can. We get to appreciate our mobility and abilities to exercise because some people wish they could, but they physically are unable to. For me, the more I exercise, the better I feel, and the better I feel, the more I accomplish. It's such a great shift to grow from viewing working out as a punishment to a privilege. Challenging your body enhances so many different aspects of your life. You don't have to have a gym membership or wait until next Monday; you can start moving your body right now. If you want your life to go to the next level, start to exercise. Honestly, ten minutes a day is better than zero. You'll find that the more you put effort into improving your health, the more you will want to.

Too many women look at their bodies with shame or frustration yet won't make the time to take care of their bodies. Once you dip your toe into the world of movement, you will start to gain the confidence in doing so many other things. Loving yourself means you take care of yourself, and the more you take care of yourself, the better you feel and the deeper your self-respect grows. You deserve to feel good. You have to decide you're worth it and commit to working on you for you.

It's not easy to feel out of breath and insecure. It's not sexy to feel gross, bloated, and heavy. It's not fun to wonder if you'll fit in the airplane seat. It's not cool to cover your legs up in the heat of summer because you feel insecure about your heavy legs. It's totally uncool to battle blood pressure issues or blood sugar issues.

Guess what, sis? A lot of those things are going to disappear when you start to prioritize your health and start exercising right now with what you can. Grab a soup can in each hand and do some weightlifting. Sounds funny and simple, and it is. Have fun with your body. Whether you are already fit or you need to release excess weight, you are worthy of gifting yourself the rewards of exercise.

What will it take for you to commit to yourself? Let me get real with you for a minute here. Do you really want to hide in the family photo because you're embarrassed of your size? Aren't you done wondering if your butt will fit in the restaurant booth? Are you willing to miss out on family fun at the beach because you refuse to put on a bathing suit? Are you going to let fear of failure or not knowing what to do prevent you from starting some sort of exercise program?

Come on! You deserve more than that. Your life will change the second you commit to putting more effort and care into yourself and who you desire to become. Why wait any longer? Today is your day to declare your commitment to creating the best body you've ever lived in. Act from a place of love and a desire to be healthier, and pray for freedom from self-loathing behavior, excuse making, and the temptation to overeat.

You've got this, gorgeous! I can't wait to hear from you on social media. Tag me and share your commitment right now and allow me the opportunity to cheer you on! Wahoo! As Olivia Newton-John said, "Let's get physical!"

A Prayer for Guidance

Dear God, I need extra motivation right now to take better care of my body. I want to feel more energized, and I need to take better care of myself. I am ready and willing to start taking responsibility for my health in a whole new way. Please help me find the inner motivation to exercise and to move my body. Thank you for all of the blessings in my life. I value my health, and it's time to improve it. Amen.

CHAPTER 11

Confession: I Flirted with Change

Change is a word that stirs up different emotions in all of us. Some people resist it, and others embrace it. As I tell my son, change is the only guarantee in life. Things will change due to age, relationships, opportunities, death, and so on. We as individuals have to learn how to accept change and adapt to it if we want to live healthy lives. It's been my experience that endings lead to new beginnings, and I believe in the saying that when one door closes, another one opens as if by magic. There's something exceptionally liberating in surrendering to change with a mindset of possibilities. How do you feel about change? Are you open to new possibilities, or do you cling tightly to what's familiar out of fear? Self-awareness is vital to creating new habits. Facing the unknown can be scary for many people because they assume the worst. What if you started paying attention to what triggers the instant fear of uncertainty in you and then started managing the trigger? How would that improve your life, not to mention your blood pressure?

There is a similar energy in excitement as there is in nervousness. I remind my clients of this often when they present with anxiety over an event. You get to tell your body what you're feeling through thought control. It's not as complicated as it may sound. It's all about creating conscious habits through increased self-awareness.

The greatest self-care practice you will ever develop is building your positive mindset. When you consciously shift how you think about change and start to flirt with the idea of what is possible you lessen the heaviness of uncertainty. I, personally, love change. It has taken many years of continual inner work to get to that level of excitement but I am there. Reframing how I thought about endings of relationships, jobs, and seasons in my life opened up so many doors to possibilities. Try it out for yourself. Let change become your favorite "c" word. Focus on growth, evolution, and possibilities and embrace situations as lessons and opportunities to become a healthier version of yourself. Is it easy? No. Is it challenging at times? Yes. You're human; your mind will cling to old beliefs and thought patterns and will definitely pull you back to old behavior when you're triggered by past events, *but* changing all of that is possible too. You grow as you go. It's a conscious choice to commit to expanding your mind and focusing on positive self-talk, visualizing a healthy lifestyle and relationships.

I am living proof of the power in positivity and growth mindset. I didn't have parents, or teachers, or anyone else in my life teaching me about all of these concepts. I sought it out on my own. I am innately wired to see possibilities in problems, but as far as choosing to increase my knowledge on this topic, I had to research the neuroscience of growth mindset and intrinsic motivation. I'll never stop. I am always learning. I took a lot of psychology courses at the college and university level and have extensive training and education in this field, but again, knowledge is only power if you take action. I have witnessed dramatic results in clients and friends who have implemented strategies to rewire their thoughts. It is so rewarding to see firsthand the power in positivity and abundant thinking. It's a total lifestyle change. It's a choice. You can decide today to change yours or stay the same; it's entirely up to you.

If this is a new concept for you, or if it sounds too good to be true, do yourself a favor and take the time to download, watch, and listen to videos and podcasts about the topic. Buy books that explore the power in thoughts and take time to absorb all of the information. I know some people have found all the information available overwhelming because there is so much of it. I suggest you chunk it down and begin with the basics. Keep it simple. Start with mindfulness. Pay attention to what you're thinking. Get focused on positive, upbeat thoughts. Think about what you are thankful for. Think about what you want to do. Get intentional about your thoughts. I also highly recommend you invest in a mentor who can support you on your journey.

The best teachers I have had on this subject are Louise Hay, Abraham Hicks, and Bob Proctor. Louise Hay's teachings on the power in language and her affirmations to heal our bodies have completely transformed my life. Discovering Abraham Hicks's teachings was a Godsend. Listening to Esther Hicks channel Abraham has blown my mind more than once. Those teachings are all about vibrational alignment. Bob Proctor explores our thinking patterns and describes them as paradigms, also known as subconscious conditioning. His teachings are based on Napoleon Hill's teachings that date back to 1937 when *Think and Grow Rich* was originally published. If you have not read that book, buy it now. It has the power to completely change your life, your relationships, and your bank account. Do not pass go; buy it! There is no excuse not to explore these concepts because there is so much free, valuable information at the tips of your fingers. Google these three teachers, open your mind to growth and expansion at a level you never have before, and commit to learning. Study their teachings for ninety days, consistently, and watch your entire life transform right before your eyes.

I remember the first time I shared an Abraham Hicks training with my mother. I recall her looking a bit perplexed, but the more she listened, the more she absorbed. Same with my son and husband; they are used to hearing me play these videos regularly, and talking about alignment is normal verbiage in our household. I know some of you are already studying these teachers and their teachings, and some of you will label them woo-woo. Anything that can change your life is not woo-woo, it is "Wahoo!" Change your perspective and change your life. There is power in possibility, and taking responsibility for your thoughts, actions, and results is the change you must make if you truly want to live out your potential and enjoy your best life.

You have options now to completely shift your life from where it is to an entirely new state. You no longer have to stay stuck in fear or worry that things will go wrong. You can learn to accept that if you try something new and it doesn't work it is okay. It is not the end of the world. If you are forced to change due to the loss of a loved one or financial issues you can shift your thoughts from fear, anger or resentment to acceptance. Take it one day at a time and don't put unnecessary pressure on yourself. You must decide what type of life you want to live. You have to evaluate your relationships. The time is now, and the results depend on you. Flirting with change was scary for me, too, in the beginning. I'd have moments where I was totally enthralled in the personal development game, yet my entire circle of influence at the time was not. Do you know how out of balance and alignment that felt? It was both unnerving and exciting. Why? Because it allowed me to have conversations with those people about what I was doing in my life. I started talking with my husband about where we wanted our marriage to go, and together we committed to improving every aspect of it and focused on being the healthiest versions of ourselves so we could experience an exceptional marriage together. I started exploring possibilities with my mother. I was able to encourage her to think differently and to really look at all she had accomplished in her life. It began to transform the experience of our time together. I quickly learned who was not available for these types of newfound conversations, and as a result of those discoveries, I decided my circle needed to change. It sounds simple, but believe me, it was next level so not simple at the time because I overcomplicated it. I addressed this in my book *PRIMETIME Success*. I included an exercise to help you figure out your own circle of influence and how it impacts your life and relationships. When I brought this up to my husband, he was very supportive of the new boundaries I needed to implement, and in fact, it got him thinking about his own family and friendships. Remember, who you spend your time with matters; this includes co-workers, clients, and social media connections.

Going through that evolution process with my husband was necessary to get us to where we are today. When you start to live what you learn, you have more changes to make. One partner cannot be growing while the other stays stuck; it will not work. You'll notice this in your parenting too. You will experience a different relationship with your children when you stop personalizing their behavior and start to accept them as they are. You will parent more effectively because you won't be stuck in the feeling of them not listening to you as your problem. You will detach from their attitudes and eye rolls and understand that your mood and energetic alignment is up to you. Essentially, you'll stop blaming other people for your experiences in life. Now, doesn't that sound sexy?

The best prescription for fear of change is to do whatever is holding you back anyway. I often talk about being fearless, and I have femme intrépide tattooed on my arm for a reason. It is there to remind me of who I am and whose I am and that I have committed to feel the fear and do the things I need to do regardless. I created a program called Fearless: 21 Days to Make Shift Happen for this exact reason. When you feel the fear and do the thing anyway, *everything* changes. You realize how caught up in the fear story you were, you do the thing, whatever you wanted to do, and you build confidence in yourself. Around here, we call that *winning*! Then you apply the same strategy to the next goal and the next goal and so forth. That is how you change your life. You choose to. Being fearless does not mean you never experience fear; it means you acknowledge it and do whatever you want to do, regardless of the fear. Essentially, you reclaim your power. I, personally, live by the motto that if it scares the *you know what* out of me, I must do it. I refuse to live a mediocre life because I was created to be PRIMETIME. I consciously choose positive what-if scenarios and acknowledge any fears that pop up and continue moving forward anyway. I assure you; it is not always fun but it is always worth it. I have committed to living a faith-based life. I am unavailable for anything else.

A lot of clients I've worked with have benefited from applying this motto to their lives too. A great example is public speaking. Do you know how many amazing public speakers, motivational speakers, and educators feel terrified to step on the stage in front of people, but they do it anyway, and they do it well? Why do you think they perform so well? They consciously visualize their success. They focus on their impact. They choose to do it scared.

What would you do right now if you stopped living in the fear of the unknown and other people's opinions and started believing in yourself and abundant possibilities?

When will you realize that you create your reality and the fear is a way of your mind protecting you from potential failure? When will you recognize the power in the "f" word? The f word, of course, being failure. So many people struggle with that word. I don't. I call those experiences fail-ups. I have tried things that flopped. I have asked for support and been told no. I have pitched my book to stores and never received a reply email. I have received rejection letters saying I needed an agent to get my book inside their store. I have emailed podcasts to be a featured guest and been ghosted. I've pitched myself to TV shows to be a featured guest and never heard back. I finally landed my own TV show because I persisted. I am relentless in pursuit of my desires. I know what I want, and I believe in my ability to have it at such a profound and deep level that I keep going. It may look like I'm lucky to some, but trust me, it is not luck. It is a relentless inner drive to be, do, and have all that I desire. I have faced so much rejection it isn't even funny. What keeps me going is my hunger to be all God created me to be. I firmly trust in God's plan for my life, and my job is to be a faithful servant. I don't have to like everything I'm called to do, but I do need to trust there is a purpose for it. I don't even have to know how things are going to work out. My responsibility is to consistently show up and do the necessary work. I understand that with increased visibility and openly speaking my truth, I am vulnerable and at risk for verbal attacks from family, friends, and strangers on the internet. I don't care about that as much as I care about fulfilling my God-given calling and being true to myself.

I have developed a daily mindset practice that includes prayer, gratitude, journaling, reading, and exercise. It's my primary self-care practice, and it has allowed me to experience life on a whole new level and continue to attract abundant blessings, people, and opportunities into my life. I choose every day to share my message, regardless of who likes it or supports it. God didn't give me this vision for my life without reason. Think about it! We all have our own unique desires and aspirations. Some of us are authors, some nurses, others teachers, and so forth. We have different desires and purposes for our lives for good reason. I don't know about you, but I do not mess around with the big guy. I trust that the vision I have been given is right for me, so I refuse to quit. Has it been scary? Heck, yeah! Have I lost money along the journey, investing in not-such-a-great-fit mentors, coaching programs, or business ideas? You know it. Have I cried myself to sleep? More than once.

Will I quit? Never.

I have built such a positive and powerful mindset and belief in myself that being ignored or told no does not alter how I see myself, nor does it scare me. What scares me is settling for good when God created me for great. It's a vibe and it all started with a decision to explore what else was possible. I want that for you. I want you to wake up to what's available to you and stop succumbing to the fear and anxious thoughts that haunt you. There is so much more waiting for you on the other side of fear. You can break the pattern of worry. You can step up and step out into an even better version of yourself. You can experience bliss on a level you have never imagined. Life gets to be fun and full of pleasure if you want it to be.

You are not defined by your past. You are not limited by your mistakes. You get to choose every single day who you want to be, and you get to work on becoming the best version of yourself.

Do not waste that gift. Do not stay stuck in fear or guilt or shame. Break free and commit to living better than you ever have. Play with the possibilities ahead for you. Start thinking about what you really want to be doing with your time. If you want to, you can completely overhaul your life. Choose to explore your potential and stop fueling your self-imposed limitations. Stop living as a prisoner to your fear. You are so worthy of experiencing life in a better way.

It starts with changing your mindset. It starts with you. It starts with a decision.

A Prayer for Guidance

Dear God, I am worrying about things that are out of my control. Please help me think positive thoughts and allow me to release the negative thoughts that create fear in me. I am ready to trust myself more. I am ready to live differently. I need a miracle. I ask you to cleanse my heart and mind of anything that no longer serves me. Thank you for all of the blessings in my life. Use me to be a blessing in the lives of others. I am open to receiving your vision for my life. Amen.

CHAPTER 12

Confession: I Started to Honor the Woman I Want to Be

If you don't change how you think and behave, nothing for you will change. After reading the previous chapter, can we agree that statement is valid? Yes? Why then do a lot of women struggle to change their thoughts and behavior? If you know that you have to do something different to get different results, then why don't more of us achieve our goals and make the changes we need to make? Is it possible that more often than not, women feel inadequate or undeserving of the things they desire? It's time for women to stop biting their nails waiting for approval and take the leadership role in their own lives. That means you, gorgeous!

I have done so much inner work to release the desire for approval from other people. When I reflected on my life choices and the consequences that came along with them, it hit me, hard! I was being the nice girl, and it was choking the life out of me. In order to honor the woman I want to be, I have to release anything that is not aligned with who she is. I spent so much of my life sacrificing my goals in order to please everyone around me. The only evidence I had was that as long as I was a good girl, a nice girl, I would be liked. You know what was missing though, all those years? I did not like myself. I was trapped. In fear, in resentment, and in confusion. I was not doing the things I wanted to do. Isn't that how good girls live? Good girls then grow to become angry and empty women. Why? Because they've been conditioned to put their needs and desires aside to ensure everyone else gets what they need, first. There is nothing left for themselves, but they get the title of good girl and nice woman. The greatest insult to me is when someone says I am nice. Nice to me equates to doormat. For all the times, as a young girl, I was taught to swallow my feelings and be nice to people who were abusive to me, I refuse to honor that word now as a grown-ass woman. Nicey nice is over!

I have compassion for any of you who are still sorting through the reasons you feel you need approval from anyone other than yourself. You will eventually get there. You will start to recognize how unnecessary it is to shove your feelings and desires down in order to be accepted by others when you start to accept yourself, fully and completely. I pray you come to realize that your worthiness is not dependent on anyone's ability to see your value. You are worthy and you belong because you do. Period. No ifs, ands, or buts about it. If I may suggest anything to get you started right now, it would be to create your own self-care practice that includes being still, closing your eyes, hand on your heart, and simply visualizing what the woman you want to be looks like. Can you see her? Is she smiling? Does she wake up energized? Is she fit? How does she dress? Is she wearing makeup? Dangly earrings? Or is she more relaxed, wearing a bun on top of her head, clear skin, bright white teeth that match her big-ass smile? Whatever you see, write it down. You get to decide what your next-level best version of yourself looks like, and there is no right or wrong. Let this be fun. Let this exercise awaken your inner goddess. She's been hiding for far too long, and she's ready to step out into the world and fly free.

I have done that visualization exercise many times. As I invest in myself and my business, I continually tap into my source connection and vision for my life; that includes connecting to the woman I am and who I want to become. I created a personal development self-care practice well over a decade ago and really tightened it up about six years ago. I continue to focus on what I need to feel and function at my best as I step into the woman I desire to be. I will never be done evolving and therefore, my commitment to always becoming healthier and better will never stop. It's a daily practice, not a one and done. I have figured out that there is always a next level. Yes, you can be content with where you are at on your journey, of course. There is power in appreciating the work you put in. However, there's always going to be opportunities for growth. Everything that happens in our lives is happening in order for us to grow and to learn. One cannot become wise without hardships, challenges, or success. Wisdom comes from doing. I don't know about you, but I am a wise woman, eager to learn and share even more with others in this lifetime.

Dr. Joe Dispenza was quoted saying, "People wait their whole lives for something outside of them to change how they feel inside of them." And that quote hit home for me. How does that make you feel reading it right now? Does it hit home for you too? Have you been prolonging your happiness in life because you are waiting for external validation from others? Is there somebody in your life that you wish would give you more respect, attention, or recognition? If yes, explore why. Why do you crave those things from someone? It is safe for you to acknowledge why, and it is safe for you to accept you may never receive such things from that person. That is how you start to be able to let it go. When you start to let things go, you realize that other people can never make you feel whole, worthy, or desirable. That stuff all comes from within. You get to give those gifts to yourself.

Whether we like to admit it or not, we have all waited on another person's approval. In fact, we learned how to do just that when we were little girls. Let's call it out; we waited on approval from our fathers, which some of us never received. We waited on approval from our mothers, which, again, some of us never received, and for some of you, no matter what you did, your mother never approved and probably never will. It can be much of the same in regard to siblings, teachers, sports coaches, Girl Guide leaders, people of the church, 4-H Club mentors, friends, and now sadly, we sometimes get caught up in seeking approval from strangers on the internet.

I, personally, had lived in the undesirable shadow of others for far too long. It may seem impossible to those who know me now, but I wasn't always this confident in myself. Far from it. I spent so much time being seen and unheard because I was terrified of never being good enough. I was an insecure child and was teased most of my childhood by family and peers at school, and I never really fit in. When you're that age, you don't appreciate being different, and you certainly don't recognize the value in it. Now I live differently. I am me. Like guacamole, I am extra, and I know it. I own my badassery in a way that parts the water of the sea. That's all I can sustainably be. I no longer identify with other people's projections on who I am or how I should live. It took work, a lot of work, but it was well worth it. Again, it's not a one and done. I still have moments when I need to sit my butt in the chair and remind myself of who I am and whose I am. Thank you, Lord, for always having my back! Jesus took that wheel many years ago, and I trust in my divine calling and use my extra-spicy personality to fulfill it.

I have been told so many times in my life that I'm too loud, too opinionated, too much, and guess what? I love it that way. I'd rather people see the real me than live in a shadow of my whole self. Like it or lump it, as my dad would say. I am who I am, and I love myself. I want that for you too.

When you wholeheartedly accept who you are—the good, the crazy, and all the things—people who cannot do that themselves will be offended by you. It's not about you, really. It's about them and their lack of self-acceptance, so why torture yourself with trying to be good enough, seen enough, heard enough, or whatever kind of validation you may seek?

When you tap into your desires, you allow yourself to explore all that is possible for you. You get to, guilt-free, imagine having everything your heart desires and then go after it and have it. True bliss! Honestly, what is better than unconditionally loving, accepting, and believing in yourself? That, in my opinion, is ultimate success.

Let's have some fun. Close your eyes and visualize the marriage, the family, the relationships, the sex life, the body of your dreams, the hair, the skin, the lashes (yes, I went there!), the wardrobe, the shoes, the car, the home, the furniture, the travel, the pleasure you want to have and/or experience. What does it look like to live your luxurious life?

Who do you have to become to experience all that you visualized? What is stopping you from creating the life and relationships you want? Is it fear? Is it lack of money? Is it your unhealthy relationship with food? Whatever you come up with is an excuse. Now, wait a minute, wait a minute! I can hear you now. "But, Christy, my list of reasons is not a bunch of excuses; they're legitimate. They're real."

No, they are not, sis! That's just you fighting for your own limitations, and I am not available for that. No matter what season of life you are in right now, there is opportunity for change. Step by step, you hold the power to transform your life. In order to become the woman you want to be, you must let go of your self-imposed limiting beliefs and ideas. Will you accept that responsibility? Will you commit to entering a new chapter in your life? A chapter where you trust the author because you are writing the story?

Start by visualizing what you want and how you desire to look; then focus on the feelings. How do you feel about your healthy body? How do you feel about your amazing marriage and sex life? How do feel about your luxurious lifestyle? Get to know the feelings in your body and do all the things you can to feel that way right now. Get lost in all the good vibes and positive thoughts and feelings and watch how quickly you start to attract good things and positive opportunities into your life. One of the greatest roadblocks I see women face is the realization that nothing is out of reach. Some of you might feel good right now – that is incredible. What would feeling great mean for you? You can learn how to love yourself more while you already do. Your feelings matter. Your feelings either allow or block abundance into your life. Feeling guilty about wanting more if you already enjoy the life you have is messing with your flow.

It seems trite, but it is all about the feeling. You will have learned this if you study the teachers I mentioned in the previous chapter. Close your eyes and imagine yourself looking like the woman you envision and living the lifestyle you desire. Doesn't it feel good? Visualize your next-level body. Write your dreams down as if they've already happened. Use journal prompts like "I am, I have, I am thankful for …"

You hold the power to speak your life into existence. Don't delay. You have waited long enough. You did not read this book by accident. These visualizations and other self-care practices and exercises will change your life. Open up to receiving all of the greatness God has in store for you. Believe that things will turn around for you, and they will. This is a new day for you. You must claim it as such. Sudden breakthroughs are going to happen. You are going to start to feel different. It may be odd at first because the power in positivity is profound. You will feel like a whole other person because you are becoming one. Like a snake sheds its skin, you, too, will shed old thoughts, old beliefs, old patterns of being. This is magical, and it is real.

Now, on this journey, you will have to take a stand for your new self. The people around you may not like your new attitude or the changes you are making. They may start to feel uncomfortable about your progress. This is where your superpower kicks in—the superpower of focus. You must decide to stay focused on who you want to be and not allow past choices to limit your new beliefs. You will have to re-evaluate your relationships and be mindful of who you are influenced by both online and offline. Becoming your best self takes work, and it takes courage. When you declare your personal power over your life, you will be tested. It's like the universe is asking you, "How badly do you want to change?" This is your moment to raise your hands in the air and swing them around like you just don't care, saying, "I've got this! I believe in myself, and I am becoming the woman I want to be." With that kind of vibe, everything you desire and more will be drawn in to you. Energy is not to be messed around with. Part of this process calls for you to take action in regard to your exercise, language, thoughts, and attitude, but the other necessary ingredient is for you to surrender. You have to trust that all things happen in divine timing, and if you consistently visualize, write, and speak your desires while taking action, they will come into fruition. You are on the edge of change, and great things do come to those who do the work while they wait. Trust and believe in that promise.

I have experienced this, and I know it is possible for you too. The path to becoming the person you want to be is preparation for when the time comes that you receive everything you have asked for and worked for. Taking care of yourself requires commitment and focus. It also requires unconditional love. You will have moments when you doubt what is possible for you. You will have to have tough conversations with your loved ones during this transformation. You will catch yourself falling prey to old thoughts or worries. You must rise up and speak your truth over them. You must believe so deeply in your abilities to create your life that fear has no power over your faith.

Read this chapter as many times as you have to, build up your physical energy to persevere with adequate sleep, and feed your mind with positivity. You've got this, gorgeous. It's time for you to show the world who you truly are. Claim it now. Say it with me: "I am beautiful. I am healthy. I am an energetic match for all that I desire. I am blessed beyond my wildest dreams. Everything I desire desires me." Blessings to you on this next-level journey.

A Prayer for Guidance

Dear God, I am ready to become the woman you created me to be. I know that everything that has happened in my life has been for a reason and a purpose. I am ready to forgive myself and love myself unconditionally. Please help me see the greatness within me. Allow me to see what you see for my life and help me become the woman who fulfills my calling. Thank you for giving me this incredible opportunity to step fully into the woman I want to be. With you by my side, I know anything is possible. Thank you. Amen.

POWER THOUGHTS FOR PHYSICAL WELL-BEING

I am nourishing my mind and body with restful sleep.

I am grateful for my beautiful body.

I love feeling fit and fierce.

I appreciate and love my body.

I have pure love for myself.

I exercise because I love my body.

I respect myself, and it shows through my behavior.

I commit to living my best, most abundant life.

I am energized and full of love.

I am so happy in my skin.

I radiate good health.

I am so confident in who I am.

I love myself as I am on my journey to becoming more.

I am healthy, strong, and fit.

I am choosing healthy thoughts that heal my body.

I am full of energy and positivity.

SEXUAL
HEALTH + BLISS
SELF-CARE

CHAPTER 13

Confession: I'm a Hot Dish

According to the urban dictionary, a hot mess is "when one's thoughts or appearance are in a state of disarray but they maintain an undeniable attractiveness or beauty." I'm not sure if there is any real definition for a hot dish in regard to where I'm going here, but what I'm trying to say is I like life *spicy*, and I'll never apologize for that.

I was originally going to title this chapter "Shitty Sex Changed Me," but I didn't know if that would reflect the significance of this chapter. I'm writing about some personal growth here, using a next-level conversation for women everywhere who hide their beauty, feel less than confident in their own skin, and are still keeping the lights off when they go down under. I am focusing on body confidence and how it impacts *everything* in our lives in this chapter, and really, who wants to read about shitty sex? I mean, if we are being honest, we have *all* experienced shitty sex. Unfortunately, one of the reasons why women experience unfulfilling sex is because they're afraid to a) be naked in front of their partner, b) tend to not know or ask for what they really want, and c) tend to resist exploring with different positions because they don't want to have a roll or muffin top or are worried about whatever else they think will show if the lights are on. Meanwhile, their partner isn't even thinking about any of those things.

The number one reason women have had or are, heaven forbid, still having shitty sex is due to low self-esteem, poor body image, and fear of speaking up and asking specifically for what they really want. There's still a bunch of mixed messages out in the world about "that type of woman." Women are expected to be hot, fit, sexy, and willing to be wild in bed, but the unspoken rule is that they just do what their partner wants, and that's that. Women, until recently, have not been encouraged to be open, experimental, or too sexual. Don't even get me started on the spiritual woman. Apparently, some think the woman who worships God and lives a faith-based life should not be a sexual being. I mean, wake up, people! God want us to experience pleasure. Why do you think our bodies are created with nerve endings in all the right places? Women can be both spiritual and enjoy great sex. The woman who is unapologetic about her faith is so deeply connected to who she is and understands that pleasure in all things is her birthright. There is no shame in being who you are and asking for what you want and need in or out of the bedroom, or kitchen, or shower, or …. you get the point.

We are exposed to media images that have been filtered and photoshopped at least twenty times that tell us what we should look like to be desirable. We can pick up a magazine, scroll social media, or watch a commercial on TV and be inundated with fake images of what women are supposed to look like and how they are to present themselves. No wonder some women stay stuck in shame. Unless you watch a Dove commercial you are not seeing real beautiful women's bodies. When will it stop?

When we collectively stop buying the products being sold with fake images, when we stop tolerating it, when we stop consuming it, when we stop allowing an image to make us feel less than. All of the above!

I'm going to spotlight numerous reasons why loving yourself and your body as it is means life-changing behaviors and decisions. It's time to declare no more war between you and your body. It is time for peace.

> She was appealing for numerous reasons,
> She was unpredictable in her familiarity.
> She juggled her emotions, like she did the household laundry.
> Alone.
> Nobody was her, and that was her selling feature.
> Only, she didn't know it.

One of the most important reasons I'm being completely vulnerable in this book is because I know there are women out there who have gone through or will go through all the things I have. I'm talking body image struggles, weight gain and loss, disordered eating, dysfunctional family stuff, breakups, heartache, loss, death of a loved one, death of a parent, divorce, single mom life, remarrying, new in-laws, work drama, starting your own business, trying something completely new and out of your comfort zone, arguments with your children, moving to support a partner, losing your temper, feeling lost, sleepless nights, health concerns, money ups and downs, and everything in between.

Women, more often than men, struggle with self-esteem issues. Why this matters to me is because I, personally, know what it feels like to fight with yourself on a regular basis because of lack of confidence and poor self-image and how it impacts every facet of your life. If you cannot receive pleasure in one area then surely, it will be difficult to experience pleasure in other areas.

I also know what it feels like to flip the coin and wake up speaking positively to yourself, to look in the mirror and love and appreciate your body. To stop being defined by cellulite or stretch marks. To actually look at your body with respect and admiration. It's an entirely different existence!

A woman who operates at her highest capacity, connected to her worth, aligned with her innate wisdom, knowing who she is inside out, will be a magnet for love, success, and a fulfilling life, including a fulfilling sex life. Our sexuality and divine feminine energy are powerful. Isn't it time you started to embrace who you are and what you look like instead of resenting it or criticizing yourself? When women stop shaming themselves for not being a certain weight or for having a few wrinkles, or for not having it all together all the time, *their* lives change. Stop wasting your time and energy striving for perfection. It makes your lady parts shrivel up and dry out. Your weight does not determine your sexuality and confidence is a vibe not a size.

You will experience some or all of the above, perhaps under different circumstances, but there will be a similarity in regard to emotions, thoughts, behavior, patterns, and ultimately the habits that lead us to eventually take better care of ourselves. Let's be honest: nobody is interested in sex when it hurts. You need to recognize where you need to upgrade your self-care game way before anything forces you to. I want all of you to understand how important you are and that the things you experience or do don't define who you are right now, and they certainly don't cap who you can become. The moment that this clicks for you is the moment your entire life changes for the better—the moment when you look in the mirror after a snotty-nose cry with mascara running down your face and vow to live differently. That moment, and you will have more than one, is pivotal. Pivotal, I say!

Say it with me: "I'm a hot dish, and I embrace the woman I am today on my journey to the woman I am becoming."

When you realize you deserve better for yourself, everything shifts. When you acknowledge your feelings instead of running away from them or avoiding them like the flu, you will never be the same. Pinky promises and high-fives all around. When you accept that you are who you are, quirks and all, and trust there's nothing wrong with you, you are essentially adding years to your life. You're entering the stage of life where pleasure becomes your new expectation in all things, life and business.

Whatever you go through, you must grow through. You won't come out of the situation the same woman. It's the law. These life events allow you to explore what you need to feel better. You start to make different decisions because you have to.

Sis, you deserve to thrive, not just survive or get by. You have no idea how incredible life can be, and that includes experiencing great orgasms and receiving more love than you have allowed into your life. Your body is waiting for you to fall in love with it. Appreciate it, moisturize it, treat it well. It's time to connect with your body on a level you haven't yet.

When I feel like too much needs to get done, or too many people want me to commit to something, or when I start getting snappy with my favorite people, I know I need to up my self-care game. That's my sign I need to let go of something and chill. It's also a time to tap into some fun sexual energy and connect with myself and my partner. Did you know built-up sexual energy creates irritability and frustration and repels manifestation?

Time to bring your sexy back!

I reflect on my experiences and look closely at whether or not I am saying yes only when I want to, if I'm fully present, in the moment with the people I love, or if I am functioning on autopilot, reacting out of past conditioning and unconscious expectations. When things start feeling overwhelming, I can easily become Miss Spazzy-Pants, as in zero to sixty in less than two seconds. Can you relate? What are your signs that you need to slow it down and allow more pleasure into your life? How do you take care of yourself so you function with confidence and get intentional about asking for what you want? What kind of intimate connection are you craving in your life right now?

Do not apologize for wanting to feel better. Don't hide from your imperfections along the way either. Embrace them proudly. Taking care of your mental health is as important and directly linked to how you take care of your physical health.

If you're like me, sometimes your regular three-month visits to the dentist for your teeth cleaning get pushed back due to travel, or schedules, or at times even money. The same goes for other appointments. When was the last time you hung out with your gynecologist?

Now back to the whole hot dish thang. I think we're all hot messes in our own ways, and that is a beautiful realization. You are allowed to be a work in progress. Sisters, stop being so hard on yourself and lighten up. Commit to loving yourself through your growing pains and prioritize your health. Research has proven that women who orgasm regularly experience less stress. Now, that's some research I can get behind or in front of!

The quality of sleep you get matters, too. I cannot stress this enough. The number one reason women struggle with mood swings and low libido is directly related to their sleep patterns. Burning the candle at both ends is disastrous. You have to prioritize your sleep, and please do not rely on sleeping pills. Your body is hard at work while you're asleep; there are different stages of sleep, and each one has a job. While you sleep, your brain and body are being cared for. Quality over quantity. It's difficult to feel sexy and ready for action when you're exhausted and the bags under your eyes are screaming for rest.

Evaluate your current routine. Track your time. Do you have a solid sleep schedule?

Do you drink enough water? Eat clean food?

Move your body?

Pray, meditate, or quiet your mind for at least ten minutes a day?

Are you hanging out with high-vibe, positive people?

Do you have enough sex to meet your needs? (See, I like things *spicy*!)

Nobody is worth losing your inner peace over. Surround yourself with stable people who encourage you to take care of yourself. High vibes are sexy! The better you feel, the better your relationships. The better your relationships, the better your life. See the pattern? It's time to call yourself out and hold yourself accountable to be the healthiest version of yourself. The woman who doesn't hesitate to create and implement boundaries and the woman who isn't ashamed to ask for pleasure.

What do you do to keep your mind and body healthy?

Remember, you can be healing and need support from others.

You can be resilient and still be sensitive and need to protect yourself and your energy. You can be anything you want to be. As I wrote in *PRIMETIME Success*, you're living life on your timeline, no one else's.

Wanting to improve yourself or your body or up your self-care game doesn't mean there's something wrong with you; it means you are taking what you've got and growing, evolving, and improving out of love for yourself. Self-love at its finest!

Raise your standards, sis!

Celebrate yourself.

Cut yourself some lack. As long as you're trying and doing what you can, who cares if you didn't bake a pie for your children's school fundraiser, or didn't send your husband off to work with a gourmet lunch, or that you forgot your sister-in-law's birthday. All of the expectations you put on yourself trickle into the bedroom. I haven't met a woman yet, who feels frisky and guilty at the same time.

You get one go at this game of life. Start embracing your quirks and enjoy the moments. Allow yourself to be your own version of a hot dish. Essentially, that means owning your *ooze* factor. Your *fierce* factor! Whoop! There it is!

What will you start doing to appreciate and nurture your body so you experience more sexual pleasure?

Here are some ideas:

«Buy fancy lotion and moisturize every inch of your body (ask your partner for help in those hard-to-reach areas!).

«Soak in the tub with zero distractions, a few candles, and a glass of wine!

«Buy sexy lingerie and actually wear it for yourself! Add some heels and a short, sassy robe—because vibes!

«During your cycle, pamper yourself and allow your body to be respected for all that it does.

«Buy that sex toy you've always wondered about trying and explore!

«Start talking sexy to yourself and appreciate the goddess within you (even if you haven't truly connected to *her* yet, *this* is how you do).

«Book a physical checkup and take control of your birth control accordingly.

«Groom yourself or don't! Do what feels good for you!

«Eat well! Bloat can destroy any desire, especially to get it on!

«Send your partner a message outlining in detail what you want him to do to you.

Take radical responsibility for your health and your sexual satisfaction.

When you love yourself, appreciate your body, and speak up for what you want, you attract more pleasure and possibilities into your life. There will be doors that open up for you as if by magic, all because you stopped hiding who you were. Instead of focusing on what you did wrong, you will start to appreciate all that you did right. *Sizzle! Sizzle!*

What an empowering feeling to own your truth and celebrate the woman you are. It's time to rise up and own your fierce factor. Soon, you'll be experiencing that ooh-la-la pleasure you've been craving and oh so much more! You'll go from feeling weird about these things to feeling wonderful and in control. You'll stop hiding in the dark and start showing off your gorgeous body with confidence. Do not dim your light. Own that orgasm, girl! Ain't no shame to your game! Go on with your hot dish self! Your pleasure is waiting.

A Prayer for Guidance

Dear God, help me to release the shame and confusion I have been carrying with me about my body. I am open and willing to experience more pleasure in my life. I want to embrace my body and enjoy a healthier sexual relationship with myself and my partner. I am ready to connect with myself and my body in a whole new, exciting way without fear or guilt. Amen.

CHAPTER 14

Confession: I Started Having Soul Sex

Connecting intimately and physically with someone you love, trust, and respect is soothing to your soul. Sex is an energy exchange between two people. I wrote about that earlier. When you allow someone to enter your body, you are sharing the most sacred parts of yourself.

Raise your hand if you've ever experienced the inner turmoil of empty sex.

Yes, sisters, I see you. I feel for you. I also have a solution for that.

I'm calling you out right here, right now. Enough with the pretending and hiding your desires; it's time to get *real* about who you are, what you want, what you *need*, and what your mind and body respond to.

Can we have a minute of acknowledgment here? Can we all agree that women love sex just as much as men do and that doesn't make them bad? Throughout my counseling career, I've had the privilege of working with hundreds of women, and I know there is still a stigma out there. Women hide their sexuality because they don't want to be called names or degraded by their peers. Hence, the series of good girls going wild. Ahem, we all know how I feel about being labelled a good girl. I have witnessed women completely transform their relationships. I have seen women heal from traumatic sexual experiences and reclaim their bodies and sexuality in magical ways. Haven't we as women suppressed our desires long enough? There is no badge of honor in pretending to have a headache when the real truth is that you are either not comfortable in your skin or you don't feel confident in asking for what you want.

Can we all agree that it's high time we embrace our sexuality in a soulful, loving way like we do or want to do for every other part of who we are? Self-care includes experiencing great pleasure. It includes having great sex and experiencing frequent and intense orgasms without feeling shame or embarrassment that you want to. Please don't tell me you are still stuck in the mindset of "good girls only have sex to get pregnant or to please their partner." Not only will I continue to pray for you, but it makes me want to shake you. Why? Because enjoying a fulfilling sexual relationship with yourself and your partner changes everything in the world of togetherness and emotional wellness. Your body was not created for the sole purpose of pleasing others.

Sex is sex; you've heard the old adage. It's like pizza; no matter what toppings are on it, it's good. Everybody loves pizza. Bzzzzzz. Wrong, again.

Sex with depth and soulful chemistry is next-level stuff that more people need to be talking about and experiencing. As I'm writing this chapter, I'm in Florida with my family for a month. I go into the kitchen to get some water and tell my husband and son which chapter I'm now writing and what it's about. I look over at my husband, and he's grinning ear to ear, and my son says, "Oh gawd," in his most supportive voice. Sex is not a taboo topic in our home. Men need to learn how to appreciate their bodies and embrace their sexuality in the same ways that women do. I believe that healthy men and women choosing to share such a blissful experience together is empowering. After all, most people struggle with sexual relationships because they feel shame for wanting to experience pleasure. That is such a sad fact. Our bodies are beautiful, and consensual sex can be magical if you allow it to be.

Soul sex involves accepting your body just as much as it includes accepting your sexual desires. It's about connection. It involves enjoyment and fulfillment. It's not about the race to get it in and get it done. Nobody said quickies aren't fun. They can be random and intense but in order to honor and embrace your enjoyment, you need to slow it down sometimes.

To be present in the moment. To feel all the things that are happening in your body as you connect with your lover.

Do you ever just look at your husband or partner and feel the electric sizzle? If you're confused about what I'm asking, then that's a no.

Developing this self-care practice of having soul sex was interesting and exciting. I spent much of my relationships trying to please others, and so what that meant is I didn't really know what I wanted. My husband made it safe for me to openly express fantasies, desires, and of course, I held space for him to do the same. Let's be honest, we both went all in on trying them out. Unconditional love and sacred connection offer you emotional and physical security. Now, don't get me wrong. There were also uncomfortable conversations and moments in the process. That's why trust and communication are so important. Sharing your desires with your partner demands trust and safety of both parties. You can't experience pleasure at the level you desire if you're hiding your fantasies or feeling ashamed of your body. It's completely out of alignment to live that way, and your sexual relationship will suffer as a result.

When I decided to share this growth experience with the world, I felt two things: one, I questioned how vulnerable I really wanted to get; and two, I had to let go of the fear that some of you would judge me or deem this inappropriate. Healthy sex is not inappropriate; nor is it something to deny yourself. Too many women have denied themselves this type of pleasure for far too long. It's time to release the shame and stigma around sex being something men enjoy and women do out of obligation. I believe that women who have never orgasmed or been on the receiving end of a great sexual encounter are the ones who think they don't like sex. Does that make sense? How can you like something you've never allowed yourself to receive? And for the sake of acknowledging all things related to creating an amazing sex life, let's talk about masturbation. Soul sex is created through conscious self-discovery and connection. When you learn how to be fully present with yourself and receive pleasure you bring a next-level experience to your sexual encounters with your partner. You also establish a more powerful connection to source. Pleasure raises your vibration and puts you on the frequency of love. So, treat yourself to a new toy off your wish-list and get busy.

Did I really just go there? Yes, I did. If you have never been intimate with yourself and explored your own body, how could you ever know what you like or what revs you up? The sex industry is booming for a reason. There is power in self-exploration and many benefits to touching yourself. If the thought of it causes you to dry up, then it's definitely an area worth exploring on your own time and own terms. Get to know yourself, girl. When you release the belief that you should be experiencing pleasure in a certain way and actually allow your body to guide you, your entire sex life changes. There is no right and wrong. So long as it's legal, go for it! Get curious and build your confidence as you explore your body. Practice the art of being present. Allow your body to respond in whatever ways it does without judgment. Stop feeling embarrassed about your own body and sexual desires and lighten up. Self-care is all about tuning into your desires and letting go of the pressure to perform in a certain way. The more present you are in and out of the bedroom the greater depth of love you will cultivate within your relationship. Soul sex is about so much more than just sexual intercourse. It is about the whole experience of gratification.

Add to this mix, the power of authentic communication. You communicate with your sex partner in more ways than one. You can have direct conversations, you can respond with sound or touch, and you can also take control and guide your partner hand over hand. You get to do whatever you desire without hesitation because it is safe for you to do so. The great news is that your partner wants to please you just as much as you want to please them. If you're with someone who doesn't care about you and only cares about getting off, run fast. Real lovemaking, passionate soul sex, whether long and slow or hard and fast is about connection. Feeling safe with your lover is imperative to your experience being positive.

It is time for women to take responsibility of their sexual health and experiences. It's time to open up your mind to what is possible. The more confident you become with your own body, the more fun and pleasure you'll have with your partner's body. Together, you will take your sex life to a whole new satisfying level of bliss.

There is something magical about willingly surrendering your body to the hands and lips of your partner, and why wouldn't you want to experience such a magnificent connection? It is time to take matters into your own hands.

A Prayer for Guidance

Dear God, help me let go of any guilt or shame I feel about my body and sexual desires. I want to connect fully with my partner and experience more pleasure. I am ready to be more open-minded and explore what is possible. Help me to feel more comfortable and confident in my own skin. Amen.

CHAPTER 15

Confession: I Stopped Giving Out of Obligation

Have you ever met someone who takes and takes and then takes some more? It could be time, energy, money, favors, or anything else under the sun. I'm sure you don't have to think long or hard to identify someone in your life who fits that mold, do you? The difference between givers and takers is boundaries. Let's face it. We all know someone who takes more than she gives and also someone who gives more than she takes. You might be nodding your head right now as you think about that person in your life. It might even be you.

I have always enjoyed giving to others, especially those less fortunate than me. In fact, I have given to others at times when I didn't have a pot to piss in, so to speak. It's an intrinsic need to do good deeds. I feel so satisfied when I make someone smile or laugh. I feel exceptional when I help someone feel worthy and loved. When I started giving to myself in that same way, things shifted fast. Do you know that, historically, women have been taught to put everyone else before themselves? It explains why mental health issues and burnout rates are so high, right? It also explains why some women feel uncomfortable taking care of themselves. Their purpose has been ingrained to serve others to a fault. That is totally out of whack for a healthy woman. I don't believe in work-life balance, and I don't believe that giving and receiving are always aligned in relationships, but I do believe that sometimes you must give more than you get, and other times you must allow yourself to receive more than you give.

When you think about why you give so much of your time and energy to certain people in your life, what do you feel? Going back to feelings here for a minute, explore it. Do you feel happy and joyful when you're driving your children from school to home, making dinner, then rushing off to pick up the neighborhood kids and take all of them to their extracurricular activity's night after night? Are you feeling joy when you work late and come home to make dinner for your husband because he hasn't started to prep anything or have it waiting for you on the table? Do you experience joy when you spend your Saturday volunteering for your child's sport team fundraiser car wash with the two moms who always gossip about the coach's wife?

If yes, fantastic! If no, stop doing those things. Seriously, doing anything out of a sense of obligation will drain you and leave you bitter. Outsource what you can and say no to the rest. Ask another parent to drive your child or pick them up at their sports or piano lessons. Set up a carpool schedule. Share more responsibilities with your spouse. Stop saying yes when you mean no, and most importantly, let your no be no. When people tell me they live a balanced life I laugh. "How?" I inquire? How is everything fifty-fifty? It's not possible. We can strive for some sort of equality in our relationships and responsibilities, but nothing is ever perfectly balanced. It's not how life works. At least, it's not how my life works and I stopped striving for it. I spent many years trying to create some sort of balance between my family life and work life, and it left me feeling bitter and exhausted. Why strive for the impossible I thought? Instead, I got intentional with my time and focused on creating family life and work life flow.

Did you know that women tend to create a lot of their own negative stress simply because they refuse to say no? Don't be that woman. It's not a desirable way to live. Release yourself from obligation and allow yourself to receive as much as you give, in and outside of the bedroom. Yes, ladies, a great sex life is a piece to the less stress puzzle. Women who actively enjoy a healthy sexual relationship with their partner sleep better, live longer, and tend to experience more pleasure overall. How can you feel sexy and desirable when you are running yourself ragged day after day? You can't; it's not possible. You feel exhausted and unappreciated instead. That's not so glamorous and fun now, is it?

Your intuition, if you listen to it, will guide you to slow down and take more time to enjoy things in life at your leisure. Being busy is interfering in your manifestation game too. It's time to introduce more play and more pleasure into the mix. Look at your day-to-day activities and see where you can cut out more time for yourself. Ten minutes here and there truly does make a difference. What would have to happen for you to feel less rushed and more confident in your calendar? Remember, there is no badge of honor for the Superwoman who forgot her cape because she was multitasking on ten to-do items at once.

Here's the thing about relaxing and receiving: if you only ever give, you eventually will grow resentful. It's human nature. If you only ever receive, you probably spend much of your time feeling entitled. Sorry, not sorry—someone has to call you out. The question is, Where is the balance in that? There is none.

I teach women how to reclaim their divine feminine goddess sexual energy and start asking for what they want in and outside of the bedroom. I do not shy away from uncomfortable topics, and I am on a mission to disrupt your normal in order to help women like you break free of the things not working in your life so that you may experience next-level living in all areas. Women deserve to be sexually empowered and fulfilled. Too many are not, and it is affecting their relationships, income, and overall well-being. Women tend to give to their partner, to their children, to their coworkers or team members, and friends, and guess who is last on their list to receive? Themselves. That's devastating. It's got to change. Re-read the previous chapter. Your pleasure gets to be your priority.

Whether it be spiritually, emotionally, mentally, physically, sexually, or financially, we have to fill our own cup first. You've heard it all before, haven't you? Put on your own oxygen mask on the airplane before your child's. But the real question is, Would you? I sure hope so, because otherwise you'd be unable to help anyone else.

Let's dive in and explore the power in giving and the results of giving too much. When you give with the intention to help or share with another, it's a wonderful experience, but if you give out of obligation, or with a hidden agenda to receive, you start to build up negative energy and emotions like resentment, anger, frustration, and bitterness. Those don't sound like fun emotions to live with, yet so many women do. When is the last time you accepted a compliment? Or allowed yourself to receive? We can over give at times when we are trying to fit in and seek approval. All that over giving does is lead to exhaustion, stress leave, and eventually serious burnout.

Burnout is the most common aging epidemic around. Nobody is talking about it, but when you over give, you are destroying the connection within your own mind and body. You start to experience disrupted sleep, you feel frazzled more often, and your adrenal glands stop working properly. If you allow yourself to get burned out, you won't be able to mentally or physically take care of yourself. You stop prioritizing clean eats, exercise is the last thing on your mind, and your sex life goes down the drain. Usually, women start to drink more wine and less water during this phase and crave more sugar and fewer greens. Everything goes out of whack all because you have been giving so much for too long. If left unattended, burnout will cause you to be unable to physically or mentally get out of bed.

Blow the whistle!

Here are some common symptoms of burnout that nobody is talking about:

- lowered sex drive
- pre-menstrual issues
- increased irritability
- IBS symptoms
- mood swings
- sleeplessness
- anxiety

The reason this chapter is focusing on the significance of receiving alongside giving is because women need to stop trying to be everything to everyone and look in the mirror. See that woman staring back at you? Who is she, and what does she need to do less of?

Your love life matters, and feeling downright exhausted and irritable messes up your game. When a woman starts to resent having sex with her husband or partner, it's too late. There are simple solutions to avoid getting to that point. Take care of yourself by establishing and implementing boundaries.

Set limits on how much time you are willing to give up and ask for help when you need it. A healthy woman knows she must do things that fuel her mind, body, and soul, and she doesn't apologize for it. She also knows that the work-life balance talk is off base, so she stops striving for the impossible and accepts that living in alignment is what's most important. She accepts that sometimes she will receive more than she has given, and other times she will give more than she receives, especially when it comes to raising children. The woman who knows her limits also knows how to respect them. She does not strive for anything but feeling good.

Healthy women understand the importance of maintaining time and energy for their sex life, and they recognize the value in connecting with their lovers. Great sex doesn't just feel good; it is good for your mind, your body, and your soul. Don't sell yourself short.

You get to have it all. A great family, great business or career, exceptional lovemaking, wonderful friendships, and the opportunity to say no without guilt or justifying it.

Cheers to satisfied, healthy women. May we be them!

A Prayer for Guidance

Dear God, lately I've been feeling overwhelmed with all of my responsibilities. Help me to manage my time better and set boundaries that are healthy for me. I want to experience more pleasure in my life, and that includes my sex life. I am ready to do life differently and be more present with my partner. Guide me, and I will follow. Amen.

CHAPTER 16

Confession: I Released the Shame around Being a Sexual Woman

Whoa! If my mother-in-law ever reads this book, she may want to skip this chapter. I mean, I am married to her son. Ahem, I feel like I could write one thousand books on this topic, but I won't write them all today. I'll get right to the point in this chapter: I accepted that being a sexual woman was healthy, and experiencing sexual pleasure is my birthright, and I want you to accept that, too.

Point: Self-care involves developing a healthy sexuality and sense of self. Sexual self-care is all about knowing yourself, advocating for your sexual health, and, yes, ladies, committing to your orgasms. There is nothing shameful about experiencing sexual pleasure when it is safe and consensual.

I grew up going to a Baptist church. The mere thought of sex before marriage was discouraged; especially, for girls. In my experience that meant you either went hog wild and explored everything you could or that you felt extreme guilt, embarrassment, and deep shame for even thinking of sex. Talk about restrictive attitudes and ultimate confusion. A lot of our beliefs about sex often relate back to clearly defined gender roles and upbringing.

If you are not comfortable in your own skin, then you'll understand the physical barriers that can wreak havoc on not only your sex life but more importantly your sexual health. For a lot of women, making a yearly appointment with the doctor is petrifying. Many women put it off and tend to forget that their hormones affect their entire lives. I mean, how many of you can relate to feeling everything from sad to irritable before your cycle, and then teary-eyed and hungry during your cycle, and then horny as hell right after your cycle? Hello, estrogen and progesterone mixed with a little teeny bit of testosterone. No wonder it's so freaking hard to keep calm and carry on most days of a month. Take care of your body; that includes your thyroid just as much as it includes your ovaries. Nourish yourself from the inside out. Learn about your body like it's your new full-time job. Make self-breast exams non-negotiable. The better you know yourself, the healthier you will be and the more comfortable you'll grow to be in and out of the bedroom.

I have worked with so many women in my private practice and throughout the years in social services that flat-out refused to book a pap smear because they were uncomfortable with their body. Honestly, that is very scary. Sexual self-care is all about establishing healthy communication—first with yourself, second with your physician, and third with your sexual partner(s).

I really wanted to include statistics in this chapter of how many women never ever had a mammogram or screen test for breast, rectal, or cervical cancers that may or may not have been prevented or detected prior to having a full-blown diagnosis, but the numbers were so freaking high I cried some and then decided not to include them after all.

Ladies! You have to know your body. Every curve, every crevice, your menstrual cycle, menopause symptoms, and what is normal for *you* and what is not. As much as we are all women with the same parts, we are different. The average doctor is basing thyroid tests on a number range that a man set decades ago. If you are having odd symptoms and want a second opinion, you need to assert yourself. It's on you to speak up about your health—sexual or otherwise. If your ear hurt, you would make an appointment to get some eardrops. If you're experiencing vaginal dryness, you feel embarrassed or awkward to tell your doctor, so you suffer in needless silence. Same goes for anxious thoughts or feeling sad more often than not. Anger is another biggie (which for some odd reason has only been talked about in relation to men) that is affecting more and more women and could be an indicator of depression. There is nothing too big or too small to share with your health practitioners. I want more women to rise up and take radical responsibility for their health.

I was facilitating a sexual health workshop for survivors of abuse a few years ago, and I remember one woman in the group told me that she took her power back by reclaiming her body and taking care of it by scheduling regular doctor appointments, doing self-breast exams, and exploring *down there* regularly to assess whether or not there were any changes. Brilliant! I cheered. I mean, what a way to feel empowered and in control of your body, right? The more connected you are with your body, the healthier you will live.

How many of you have cancelled a doctor appointment out of fear or embarrassment? Please, for the love of all things holy, make that call today. If you have a man in your life, have him do the same. Your sexual health affects *all* of you—mind, body, and soul. Do not mess with it, and do not allow any insecurities or awkwardness to put you at risk. We all have hair in random places. Get over it!

When you know your body, you can more clearly recognize when something is off, not feeling right, or plain old needs to get looked at.

Bonus, when you know your body, you also experience far more pleasure in the bedroom, the shower, or wherever else you like to *get jiggy with it*. Did I really just say that? Thanks, Will.

Your stretchmarks, whether you've been pregnant or not, are yours. They are medals of motherhood for some, and for others, they symbolize the strength your body has to gain or release weight. Appreciate your body for all it has permitted you to do; it literally transports you everywhere you go. When you reframe your body talk and start appreciating all of the things your body allows you to do, you begin to transform your relationship with it.

A lot of women ask questions about how to get more comfortable with their bodies. The answer is simple: explore it, respect it, and get to know it well. Research proves that women are far more reserved in discussing sex with their health practitioners, and if they're not discussing it with them, they're probably not discussing it with their partner or anyone else. Why is that, do you think? Why are women embarrassed to talk about sex and their reproductive organs? Why do women whisper to one another about these topics?

Could it be that for far too many decades, women enjoying sex was a taboo topic of conversation? It's not anymore, so the first thing to do is drop the shame around liking, wanting, or needing sexual satisfaction, whether you go solo or are in a duo.

Empowering women to feel good about themselves includes teaching them to embrace their sexuality. Let's get to the good stuff, shall we?

Did you know that many women have never actually had an orgasm? You may be one of them. Being a healthy sexual woman involves owning your experiences in and outside of the bedroom. There is power in an orgasm, ladies.

I'm going to acknowledge the fact that many women have faked an orgasm for their partner. Gasp! Yes, it's true. I mean, who hasn't at least once? Yup. Sorry, dudes! If for some reason, you're reading my book and are scratching your head, wondering who it could have been that pretended you were floating her boat, don't waste your time because you'll never know. We women are great actresses. (Insert fist bump here.) But why act? The only person losing is you.

Some women have faked the big O because they read something juicy in a cheesy romance novel and think they're supposed to respond in a stereotypical manner. Some women have watched another woman actress be wild and boisterous in a R-rated movie or porno and tried to replicate it (hence the word actress!), to indicate to their partner that they, too, were hot and wild. Some women fake it because they don't want to hurt their partner's feelings. Some are struggling with vaginal dryness, so sex actually hurts. And other women, well, because they have no idea what they like or what will get them there, or they want the sex to end. These are not new facts. Women have been finding reasons to minimize their sexual desires for decades, and it's time it stopped. This isn't about shaming our partners either. How can a man please us if we don't tell him what we want?

Self-care tip number one: explore your body with an open mind. You'll never fully understand the *oh so amazingness* of your body (and all those tiny little nerve endings that are in just the right spots) or in your sex life if you don't know what you like. And if you don't know, how in tarnation can your partner know? I explore that in more detail later on in this book.

Self-care tip number two: protect yourself in all the things and take all the necessary precautions if you're a) not in a monogamous relationship or

b) don't want to get pregnant or put yourself at risk for an STI (sexually transmitted infection), or for those of you my age or older, formerly known as STD (sexually transmitted disease).

Guys need direction, and a lot of it! Let's face it. Most of them have learned about sex through watching fake sex (a.k.a. pornography) or from a friend, and we all know those two sources don't touch the surface of real-time sex. PS. Your partner wants to please you. If they don't, then get a new partner.

Drop the fear, throw out the shame, and actually commit to experiencing pleasure! Step into your fierce feminine power and own your sexuality like a badass. Do not apologize for having sexual fantasies or desires. You are a beautiful goddess who deserves to experience next-level pleasure in ways you have never imagined possible. What if you really do love having sex and connecting with your partner, but you've never allowed yourself to admit it? It's time you took matters into your own hands.

A Prayer for Guidance

Dear God, sometimes I feel embarrassed about my body. I want to feel more comfortable in my skin and in my sexual relationship. Help me to release the confusion and guilt I have been carrying about wanting to experience more pleasure. I am ready to build a healthy sexual relationship with myself and my partner. Amen.

POWER THOUGHTS FOR
SEXUAL HEALTH + BLISS

I am full of sexual energy.

I am grateful for my body and the sexual pleasure it gives me.

I choose to explore and embrace my sexual desires.

I am in control of my body and choose to share it when I want to.

I communicate my sexual desires with confidence.

I am worthy of love and kindness from others.

I deserve to experience pleasure often.

I am sexually and emotionally thriving.

I am confident and comfortable in my sexuality.

My sex life is exciting and fulfilling.

I choose to prioritize my sexual health.

I have intense and frequent orgasms that satisfy my body and mind.

I feel connected to my sexual partner.

I relax and enjoy sex as I connect to my body.

I choose to release my past and open up to sexual flow with curiosity and confidence.

I say yes to sexual pleasure.

EMOTIONAL
STABILITY
SELF-CARE

CHAPTER 17

Confession: I Had to Break Up with Food

For the longest time, I was wrapped up in a secretive, destructive, and emotionally unhealthy affair.

It was my relationship with food.

I was so addicted to numbing myself out that I ate based on the emotion I was feeling and not for physical hunger. The actual term for that is emotional eating.

I don't think I actually knew what physical hunger ever really felt like. I'm not 100 percent convinced that I do now either. Thank God for that.

I used to be really mean to my body. Like, really mean. I was at war with my body and mistreated it, unfortunately, for many years. I was told throughout my childhood that I was too big and too tall for a *girl*. Then many years later came the *you're too thin* comments. I was constantly being told I was *too* something! Being anything but acceptable to others for so long messed with my feelings toward myself. Due to my slew of abandonment issues I tried really hard to be liked; deeper than that, I needed to feel wanted. It's hard to build self-esteem when the people closest to you are constantly putting you down, acting like you're disgusting, and calling you names.

My fingers aren't shaking like I thought they would as I busily type away. A secret I kept successfully for years is now out. But damn does it ever feel good, sister!

The first step in being able to release this unhealthy relationship was to let go of the shame I had carried for so long and the feelings of unworthiness associated with my body shape and size. I used to feel ashamed of my desire to eat. It was commonly known growing up that the thin and pretty girls ate like pigeons. I'm an eagle, baby, and eagles like to eat.

Before I dive into all the things, it is my intention to share pieces of this chapter of my life to help any of you who may be stuck in the middle of this horrific inner battle. May I shine light on the potential healing that is available to you and open your eyes up to the self-love and respect that are waiting for you.

Taking you back to my childhood, I was always being criticized about my body. Perhaps you can relate. I was surrounded by thin cousins and girls at school who were always more popular than me. I read *Woman's World* magazines weekly that my grandmother brought home, all of which had covers boasting the latest fat-blasting diet. Environment influences our thoughts. I know that to be true.

I heard it from the teachers, the church ladies, the farmhands on my grandparents' farm, everyone at Girl Guides, 4H club, sports team coaches, and even strangers. I was big for a girl, which essentially meant tall, but it hurt nonetheless to be treated like I was some kind of weirdo. Was I though? Looking back at childhood photos, I was not *big*. There was only ever one person who did not criticize my body, and that was my dad. My dad was a man who didn't criticize any woman's body. Period. He was one smart dude.

I can remember feeling so confused. I actually liked my body at one point. I don't recall how young I was, maybe eight or nine. I remember feeling twisted about the mixed messages I was exposed to—hearing at church that we are all God's children and beautiful as we are, then tormented by some family members who spent most of their time calling me fat. Could I be loved and worthy *as I was* when everyone around me was being so critical and hurtful about my body? I knew I was pretty because no one ever made fun of my face!

I had such a warped sense of self back then. The year I hit puberty was hell. I went from feeling confused about my body to being angry at it. I mean, I did what a lot of young girls do – played dress up and stuffed my mother's bras pretending to be a woman and laughed about it. Yet, when puberty struck me it started becoming my reality. I had boobs! Do you know what names they call young girls who develop breasts quickly? It was horrible. I was one of the only girls in my class that had started her period and I hated it. Something that is a beautiful and natural life event became a source of pain for me.

Since I'm writing this book about confessions and the self-care strategies and practices that have helped heal my perception of self and my relationship with my body, I have to tell you that learning how to love yourself is not going to happen overnight, but with consistent, positive self-talk, a commitment to living better, and clearing your environment of jerks, it will happen. It's only taken me four decades!

As we all know, a belief is a thought we continuously think over and over again. My beliefs were being shaped and influenced by the people around me, and I fell heavily into the pit of self-hate. If I hadn't had my connection to God and believed, even in that desperate time, that I was here on this earth for some purpose, who knows what would have happened. It was constant. Every day was another opportunity for someone to put me down. They called it teasing, but it was bullying. I was told that boys tease girls they like. No, that teaches absurd acceptance of abusive behavior at a young age. Please don't tell your daughters that. You are not mean to someone you like. Period.

I used to try to eat alone. I didn't want people watching me. Even in elementary school, I can remember the skinny girls, the so-called popular girls, would eat plain iceberg lettuce and carrot sticks their mothers had prepared. It made for nasty breath; you didn't want to be sitting next to one of those girls after recess. I suggest their mothers had issues? Just saying!

I enjoyed a sandwich, cookies, usually an apple or some type of fruit, and whatever else I wanted. I thought I'd hit the jackpot when I got a Lunchable. I mean, who didn't love the crackers, cheese, and salami along with the little chocolate bar? I always wanted the Kit Kat. Hot dog days and pizza days were even better when the school hosted them. I'd get my mom to order me two hot dogs and two slices of pizza. If chocolate milk was an option, I had to have it! My parents never told me to watch what I ate. It was not a conversation in our house. My family knows how to eat. We all eat more cheese than anyone I know. It's like a rite of passage. My parents never withheld food from me, ever. In fact, I was raised that children clear their plate whether they are hungry or full. So, there's that.

Writing this particular chapter has been interesting because there are many moments in my childhood I do not remember, yet any experience having to do with feeling not good enough and turning to food is prominent in my mind. Every memory of feeling useless, fat, or unworthy was linked to my body. I soothed the uncomfortable feelings with food. So, the cycle continued.

I remember feeling fat at age eight or nine. Feeling gross. Feeling out of control and not good enough for love. How sad is that? I felt bad because I liked to eat. Honestly, I embrace my inner child and send so much love to her now as an adult because I didn't enjoy life for many years because of my obsession with food and my body. I started to burry my insecurities, fears of always being the fat girl, being unwanted, the hurt feelings, and the worry of always being picked last in food. Particularly junk foods! A flakey warmed my heart, and cookies, well, they comforted my fears all while fueling my shame. Chips, well, the crunchiness brought relief from all the names I was called, and before I knew it, I had started an abusive relationship with food while avoiding feeling my feelings. Now, let's be clear. My emotional eating issue was with foods that were sweet, breads, pop, and chips. Not foods like carrot sticks or radishes. That could have led me down a different path. In my family, food was symbolic to love. Food was something that was always available to me. I didn't have to ask to have a snack. I could go to our pantry and get whatever I wanted. The only stipulation was that I showed up at the dinner table and cleared my plate. I didn't know what physical hunger was because I fed my emotions. I often cried myself to sleep and prayed that God would help me stop gaining weight. I was too young to see the connection between my beliefs, thoughts, and behavior of emotionally soothing myself with food. As I continued to grow and develop, I found much comfort in food. I ate when I was bored, upset, angry, and scared. It became a pattern. It controlled a lot of my life. I felt so embarrassed about my inability to say no to food. I wasn't saying no to other things that hurt my body either.

This went on for years and years, until I healed the parts of me that needed loving attention and self-respect. Developing a healthy relationship with food has not been an easy task, I assure you, but it has been a journey I am grateful I had the courage to take. I love my body. I really do. My body confidence is real, and I hope all of you will start appreciating your body, your legs that carry you through each day, your hips that prove you are a woman, your breasts that no matter what size are symbolic of your divine feminine energy. Women, we are sexy creatures, and it's a wonderful truth that we come in all different shapes and sizes.

As I continued to grow, so did my unhealthy relationship with food, and I went from feeling fat and unworthy to developing a full-blown self-loathing obsession. The healing journey took years, but I'm so proud of myself for never giving up. I couldn't imagine feeling how I do now back then. The secrecy, the guilt, and the shame ate at me so in turn I ate them back. There is hope. There is potential for you to have a healthy relationship with food, if you eat your emotions. Other people starve them. That's another type of unhealthy relationship with food.

Do you know how freaking exhausting it is to have to function at school, on sports teams, in the boardroom, and in the bedroom, all the while being completely fixated on your caloric intake? Man, oh man, I sometimes don't even know how I did it and continued to excel in other areas of my life. I was tired. If you have gone through this or are currently battling the inner monster, you are tired too. I'm sending you all the love and good vibes, sis. You will get through this. Ask for help.

Back when things were completely spiraling out of control, I started playing around with ways in which I could punish myself for being so gross, so unworthy of attention, and so out of control. The little girl in me who desperately wanted to feel loved, accepted, and wanted had turned to self-punishing behaviors because I was none of those things. Implementing a self-care practice focused on healthy eating was hard. It was a meal-by-meal journey. Food is not the enemy. We need to feed our bodies, and we deserve to feed them well.

My secretive relationship with food was ruining my life. I was obsessed. I was living in shame. It was such an unhealthy and frightening time in my life because it felt like I would never escape it.

I had put so much energy into this relationship that all my other relationships were suffering.

There is nothing blissful about disliking your body. I literally am tearing up now as I admit to those monstrous, all-consuming years of unhealthy eating. I live so differently now but am still easily triggered. I know some of you are torturing yourself with binge eating and live with disordered eating, but there is a better way. You have to ask for help. The greatest demonstration of self-love for me personally has been forgiving myself for treating myself so poorly based on the projections and opinions of what other people thought or said about my body. God created me in all his glory, and I am worthy no matter what size I wear and no matter what the scale tells me. I trust that and feel that deep sense of love now. I have made amends with food. It is safe for me to enjoy food. I am committed to working on my health from a place of love, not hate, and certainly free from obsession. I want that for you. I want women all around the world to embrace their bodies as they are right now. Go look in the mirror, no matter how uncomfortable that may be for you, and bless your body that appears before your eyes. Appreciate your vision and ability to see your body. Appreciate your heart that beats inside your chest without you ever having to wonder about it. Start wherever you must to respect yourself but start now. That is the only way to take your power back. Society will always have ideas about what is sexy and what is beautiful, but confidence is what's sexy. Loving yourself is what generates beauty. You have the power to change your life, and it starts with the decision to take responsibility.

I am so proud of where I am today—the inner work I've done and continue to do, the self-advocacy, the released emotional baggage, all of it.

My entire life changed when I broke the secrecy about my emotional affair with food. That pain turned into purpose when I started to use my experiences and my successful healing to help people change their lives too. It is possible! I know some of you are hurting right now or have struggled with eating disorders, and I pray that you, too, will find the inner strength to say enough is enough.

Get the proper help. Commit to healing.

As a body-positive advocate and women-empowerment leader, I need to address a few things that I know some of you have gone through, may be going through right now, or have a daughter or a niece going through.

Our bodies are beautiful and phenomenal. They truly are.

It's fascinating to think of how amazing our bodies are and what they can do. For me, that means carrying my son and delivering him into this world. Nursing him, and doing things that are legit miracles. How can I disrespect that? I go back to the wonders of my body when I feel triggered. I made a vow to love myself inside out and to appreciate all that my body allows me to do. It feels good to fuel my body with healthy foods. It feels good to look at myself in the mirror and respect what I see. God has a plan for each and every single one of us, and we deserve to feel good about who we are no matter what life stage we are at.

Sometimes we feel awkward or uncomfortable, and it feels easier to become angry with our bodies than to respect and appreciate them; they hold too much water weight, grow hair in random places, our hormones can go crazy on us, and night sweats suck, period. Some women have felt betrayed by their bodies because they cannot conceive or carry a child. The magnificence in all that we are and the natural progressive changes our bodies go through should be celebrated, not something we shame ourselves for or detest about who we are. No matter what our struggles are or have been we deserve to treat our bodies well. That means not over-eating or under-eating amongst numerous other things.

Think about it. Our bodies do all the things they need to do to survive all on their own, independently of us. We do not even think about taking in oxygen; our bodies know what to do. Our heart pumps blood through our veins without us having to tell it to do so. We digest food without even thinking about the entire process. Can we commit to loving our bodies, as they are, with the intention to nourish them and treat them with the respect they so deserve?

I was the girl in elementary school who had to wear a bra before every other girl in my class. The boys were cruel, the girls were nasty, and let's just say the more I developed, the more I started to not like my body. I was taller, bigger, and had boobs. Trying to fit in and not get bullied every single day was a full-time job.

There were so many triggers that led me to binge eat and be upset with my body. I was so mean to my body. I did other things that were completely unhealthy and destructive to my body. I smoked some cigarettes, drank way too many double-double coffees, and participated in things that were totally not aligned with who I am.

I'd feel endless guilt about food I had eaten, but it was all in secret. I'd cry tears of self-disgust and shame. I'd pinch my belly fat, pick at my face, think of all the things I detested about my body, like my muscular legs, and I'd compare myself to every other girl I knew. This lingered on well into my twenties, after having my son. Come to think of it, the only time I loved my body was when I was pregnant. I obsessively measured myself, weighed myself, and allowed the scale to dictate my mood. I was mentally exhausted from the obsession with my weight, the stretchmarks I acquired during pregnancy, and the years prior when I was growing and developing into a young woman. I would soothe myself by consuming thousands upon thousands of calories in a late-night setting, always in secret.

Can we have a moment of silence for any of you who relate to these unhealthy and obsessive behaviors? Sisters, I am sending you so much love. Whenever you get the opportunity, and there will be many, to be kind to yourself and other women, do it! We are all in this together. If you have children or know children who are struggling with their body confidence, help them. Help them see their worth.

Teach them to self-regulate without turning to food. Lead by example.

Put your hand on your heart and forgive yourself if you have ever been cruel to your body and choose to move forward. Choose right now to recommit to self-love. Commit to being the best you and the healthiest you that you can be one minute, one hour, one day at a time. My best piece of advice is let go of what isn't serving you, and that includes the heavy shame and fear. The binge drinking, the unhealthy habits, the self-destructive criticism, the overexercising, the lack of daily movement, the fad diets, the diet pills, the empty or unsafe sex, and any other abuse you put your body through. Don't rehash it all. Just commit to improvement. If you slip up, acknowledge it, reflect on what triggered it, and move forward with more knowledge of what you do want and act on it.

Sincerely, make a promise to your badass self right now to love, respect, and appreciate the woman you are and the woman you are becoming. Allow yourself to enjoy food. Activate your ability to feel your emotions instead of eating them.

You're so worthy of love, and it's got to start within. That, my fellow sister, is true self-care.

What helped me end my emotional affair with food?

1. *Acknowledging the problem.* You're thinking, *Yes, of course!* But it took many years to admit it out loud. I knew for many moons I had an eating disorder and body dysmorphia. I'm smart. I hid it very well. So, yes, acknowledging it out loud was huge in my self-care journey and, ultimately, recovery.
2. *Forgiving myself.* Releasing the shame and accepting that what led me to these unhealthy behaviors was fleeing from me, and I deserved to forgive myself for hurting my body for so long. Significant!
3. *Committing to change.* It's very difficult to go from disordered eating and calorie obsession to eating regular meals, yet that's what dieticians and nutritionists want you to do. Nope! Not for me. Committing and recommitting to changing and healing my relationship with not only food but my body made the difference. Eating disorders are all about control, really. Commit to staying the course.

There is so much healing available to you. Claim it now. You deserve to live free of emotional eating. You will overcome this, and you will experience an entirely different relationship with food. I believe in you.

A Prayer for Guidance

Dear God, I need your help right now. I am in a horrible mess between my body and food. I want to feel better. I need help from the right people. Please direct me to the appropriate resources and give me a sense of comfort. I feel so lost and run-down right now. I believe there is hope for me, and I am ready for healing. Amen.

CHAPTER 18

Confession: I Gave My Past the Heave-Ho

Throughout this book, I have been sharing pieces of my journey to help you understand that anything is possible. I am proof of that! I have created the most incredible life for myself through consistent inner transformations, and it keeps getting better and better. I share specific exercises in my book *PRIMETIME Success* that will be beneficial to you as you decide what's next for you in the game of life. One of the most important decisions you will ever make is what you decide to do with new knowledge. Will you explore what's possible for you, or will you continue to think life could never be amazing for someone like you? I came from a broken home and beat every statistic that experts put on girls like me. There is nothing standing in your way but you. No matter where you've been, you can get to where you want to go. It can feel terribly uncomfortable when you decide that you really don't like how you're living. You are required to shift from living in your autopilot state to consciously creating new habits that will shape your new identity. When you release old habits and thoughts that you've carried for most of your life, you are entering new territory.

Breaking old patterns is not for the faint at heart. It is not easy. You have to recreate yourself through your thoughts, habits, and choices. You literally have to let go of your past, who you were, things you used to do, and completely commit to being a healthier version of you. There will be ups and downs, and there will be times when you question why you're putting yourself through this transformation. You cannot go back though. Not to the chaos and the negativity. Not to the old you; you are evolving, and you made the decision to evolve for a reason. You wanted life to be different, and therefore, you have to accept that stepping out of your comfort zone will feel scary at times. The predictable you must shed her skin and recharge her energy.

There is so much greatness waiting for you. Keep going. Hire a mentor, get an accountability partner, and practice extreme self-care. Your mind will play tricks on you and make you question what the heck you are doing. It's all part of the process. Stay focused on why you want to live differently and be mindful of who you share your desires and progress with along the way. Not everyone in your circle will think it's a good idea to make decisions from soul desires. Trust me! Some will think you have gone and lost your mind, and maybe you have, but life on the other side is so much better than settling for mediocre. It's your decision. Those of us who have a deep inner calling to be somebody great and to do big things cannot be influenced by those who don't.

Oh boy! This already feels like a rant starting, but really, I want to lay it out there for all of you who are stuck or struggling with the shame, the guilt, or, heaven forbid, the regret from days gone by. The past cannot be changed, but your present choices are in your control. Take a deep breath and ask yourself, "Who am I?"

That's a loaded question. I used to answer it with all the things of my past identity—thoughts, choices, and behaviors. I thought my childhood wins and losses were who I was. I thought my education and career titles over the years were who I was. I thought I was a mom, a wife, a daughter. I used titles I was given in life and business to answer the question, and you know what? I am so much more than any of those titles, and so are you. You are a woman, first. It's time to reclaim your power and get back in the driver's seat. Who are you? Dig deep and start figuring it out. Some women I work with have zero clue who they are underneath all of the titles they wear, and it scares them to think that they have put their desires, their health, and their hobbies on the backburner for years to be all the other things people expect them to be.

I used to sit and ponder this question often when I first started my personal development journey. I had to get my head around the concept that I was able to create a new answer if I didn't like the ones I was coming up with. What a powerful concept that is when it finally clicks! It seemed to me that no matter what life event or morning journal session was causing me to ask myself this question, I consistently answered it the same way. As a woman who has journaled and written since I was a little girl, I am all about growth and reflection. I guess I felt that somehow, I was supposed to radically shift each time I explored the question and come up with a new and improved answer. I believe we are constantly facing different life events, relationship changes, loss, and so on because we must evolve. If we stay stuck in all the things of the past, we aren't closing any doors, so no new ones can open.

Choosing to become the woman I wanted to be took a lot of effort on my part. I started exploring my dreams, which I had since I was a young girl. I then looked at what I would have to do in order to be the woman that made her dreams come true. I had a lot of hurt and pain to release if I was ever going to rise up and be that kind of woman. I had a lot of emotional baggage to drop off. I had numerous relationships to end. Where to begin, I thought? I started with forgiveness—forgiving myself for choices I made over the years, forgiving others for the pain they caused me via their actions and words, and forgiving God for all the reasons I was angry at him and confused about why certain things had happened to me. I haven't always believed that everything happens in my favor. Just saying! Then, I made the most powerful decision I have ever made. I closed the door on all of it. When you come to terms with your past, you accept it, take responsibility for your role in situations, and release it. It cannot hurt you or haunt you any longer. When you close the door on it, you take away its power. You are free. It doesn't matter if someone tries to sling old dirt up and throw it at you because you have made peace with your past. You are no longer available for conversations about things that are not aligned with your vision of who you want to be. You are only available to move forward, continuously becoming healthier, stronger, more confident, and present in the here and now. The past is gone forever, so why keep the negative parts of it alive in the present moment? Some women hold themselves hostage in their own lives, waiting for an apology that's never going to be given. You have to take responsibility for your own healing and happiness.

Self-love, to me, is more about loving and accepting myself as I am and not rehashing things that cannot be changed. This confession took a long time to admit. I clung for so long to the story of being the abandoned, unwanted girl who would never be enough. It was my excuse when I hurt people I cared about and didn't want to take responsibility. I no longer wanted to fall back on old wounds. I wanted to heal them, clean them out, and move on. Emotional intelligence at its finest! Once I released that story and took away its hold on me, *everything* in my life changed. It was not a pretty process, but it has allowed me to step fully into the woman I am today. I own my badassery and my life experiences, and I love myself so deeply. Taking the personal development courses, hiring coaches and mentors, and doing the work consistently, has allowed me to be the *me* I always wanted to be. I wake up every day so grateful that I made the decision to explore what was possible for a girl like me. To some people I know, I've accomplished so much that they wonder when I'll stop. When will it be enough? I say never! It's never enough. I am committed to being the best version of me at each level of success and always looking to evolve. PS. If you are one of those people who ask me when I will be done with personal development and pursuing my dreams, I'm just getting started!

We grow, shift, and mature through each chapter of our lives. At least, we're supposed to. I know there are more changes ahead of me in order to become the woman I want to be. I also know that I must love myself along the way. I am grateful for where I am and eager for so much more. The habits that got me here will not necessarily get me to the next level of life I desire. I have really big dreams, and I refuse to quit on myself. Other people think it's too much, but my dreams were placed in my heart for a reason.

As a woman, a mother, a wife, and badass lady boss, I have indeed experienced some radical shifts through each chapter of my life thus far. I literally had to get real with myself, which is critical on any self-care journey. You cannot create the life you desire, build the marriage you want, develop a healthy parenting relationship with your children, or establish awesome relationships with your co-workers, team, and employees if you don't like yourself or the choices you're making. When you accept yourself—*all* of you—people can't hurt you by throwing past stuff in your face because when you're good with it, you're good with you. Accepting your flaws, strengths, and everything in between doesn't mean you 100 percent love them; it means you accept them as a part of you but do not allow them to define you.

When you constantly feel stuck or think about what has happened to you, or things you may have done to others, you are not free. You're literally trapped in the past. All you have is right now. There is no absolute guarantee of tomorrow, and you cannot change yesterday, so why willingly torture yourself? Stop doing things that aren't aligned with who you want to be. Start focusing your time and energy on positive things and positive people. Imagine, every single morning, you wake up actually liking who you are. What a feeling!

No matter what happened the day before, you are able to appreciate the current moment—the here and now. Imagine what would change for you—for your marriage, for your children, for your household dynamic, in your work.

Take a deep breath through your nose, and as you do, think about something that's been bugging you, something from your past that you still think about often. As you exhale through your mouth, release the thought. Ahhhhhh! Feel that pesky thought leaving your mind. This is a simple breathing exercise that you can do as often as you need to.

We all have stories we tell ourselves about situations we have been through, and because we think about them so frequently, they have become our beliefs. In that sense, I praise the good Lord that we can retell our stories, create new stories, and learn how to control our thoughts.

"I am" are two very strong and powerful words. We've been hearing that for decades from all the greats!

There is so much truth in those words, and the best part is we get to say who we are.

We get to choose what words we structure together after those two.

Wrapping your head around that concept and choosing different words will transform your life.

I encourage you to journal on this often. Write "I am" at the top of your page and list as many things that you can possibly think of. The first time you do this, don't control the words; just let them flow freely through you from pen to paper. Review what you've written and cross out anything that is not uplifting, positive, or necessarily true for you anymore.

Then rewrite your list.

I will share some examples from my personal journal:

I am an exceptional mom.

I am a loyal wife.

I am trustworthy, and I trust myself.

I am smart.

I am capable and competent.

I am funny.

I am empathetic.

I am resilient.

I am thoughtful.

I am a best-selling author.

I am generous.

I am worthy of financial freedom.

I am a badass with a good ass.

There are still moments when old beliefs or fears pop into my mind, but I am able to quickly diffuse them and shift my thoughts because of all the personal development I do and have done. I remind myself, as I will remind you now, what's past is past. Don't carry it into your present moment. I want to ask you, "Who are you?" Not just what your name is but *who* are you? What do you like? What do you dislike? What sets your heart on fire? What are your values? What are your fears? What are your dreams?

I completely believe that whatever you say you are, *you are.* Yup! Whether you think positively about yourself or not, you will feel what you think, and you will make decisions based on what you feel.

Thought -> Feeling -> Behavior

That's the order in which you live your life.

If I say I'm smart, competent, healthy, and hot AF, then I am.

Alternatively, if I say I'm fat, too emotional, and not desirable, then I am those things too.

I believe that the more honest we all are and the more we truly intend to empower fellow women, the healthier the world will be. Call it sisterhood! Call it vulnerability. Call it keeping it real. Heck, call it whatever you like. We can be, do, and have whatever we believe we can, and it all starts within. It also includes recognizing defeat on a friend's face and offering a hug without giving advice. It includes telling a sister you're there for her without telling her you fully understand what she's going through. Sometimes it about holding safe space for one another. We must rise up and support one another from a place of love, not judgment. We have been playing the comparison game for so long it's now boring. When one woman admits she has struggled or is struggling and takes action to handle her situation, it inspires other women to do the same. Let's give one another permission to once and for all be ourselves in all our hot messes and in all of our successes, okay? Pinky promise. Lock it in.

One of the poems in my book *EXPOSED: Diary of a Self-Care Junkie* is below:

A Revolution

She wanted to start something,
Like a group or community event, a vibe.
Where women could connect.
Where women felt safe and secure.
Where women were celebrated by each other.
So, she started a revolution of her own.

Stop living life through a filter and start being the real you.
Confidence and self-awareness are my two favorite things to talk about because they are super-duper important in this thing called life. Confidence is built through trial and error—essentially, learning about yourself and what you are capable of throughout each chapter of life. Confidence starts with self-acceptance and respect—owning who you were, owning who you are right now, and not worrying about your past. Without self-respect and self-confidence, you will tolerate behavior and engage in activities that do not serve you or your higher good. You'll also let yourself get away with your own bullshit. It's time you gave your past the heave-ho and, once and for all, let it go!

Let's get personal, gorgeous! C'mon. Lean in a little closer. How are you talking to yourself? If you're like me and thousands of other women

I know, you can be so harsh, so critical, and downright mean to yourself. It's scary! You will say things to yourself that you would never speak out loud to anyone else, even people who have wronged you. You know that inner BS going on in your pretty little head isn't serving you. But like a broken record, it's on repeat because, well, you've gotten used to it, and perhaps you aren't consciously aware of how to minimize it, shut it down, and shift your inner dialogue. Maybe you were put down so much in your childhood, adolescence, and even perhaps in an adult relationship that you truly don't know what the EFF to do to change it. I've got you, girl! We are whatever we say we are, and as simple as it may sound, the only way to stop the madness is to consciously choose to. Start choosing better thoughts.

Whenever you catch yourself saying something nasty about or to yourself, pause. Visualize a flashing yellow caution light in your mind and breathe. Then, replace it with something positive. Examples follow: *I'm doing the best I can. I'm a work in progress. I am raising my standards. I am deserving of success. I am beautiful. I am figuring it out.*

You get the point! A lot of the clients I've worked with over the years reported success when I suggested they visualize a flashing yellow light. It tells your mind to *pause.* You can train your mind to slow down and choose a better thought. Try it! Whatever you have to do to stop the negative thoughts, do it. After much work, frustration, exhaustion, and a commitment to getting healthier and more mindful all at once, I did it, and you can too.

Suggestions for you to create a healthier growth mindset include reading self-help books, listening to podcasts, YouTube videos, diving into prayer, and journaling. I also encourage you do mirror work. Look in the mirror and speak life and love to yourself. At first, it sounds weird and may even feel weird, but do it anyway. Start with one minute, but start. What's super important to clarify is that I still work on myself, my mindset, and my self-appreciation every single day. I continue to appreciate my body and speak love into my eyes while looking in the mirror. It takes work, it takes focus, it takes consistency, and, girl, it takes guts! It takes a daily commitment to yourself, to your growth, and to doing the actual work.

We must take control over all the lies we have told ourselves about who we are and what we are capable of. Navigating this whole self-care journey and personal development process requires you to become self-aware of all the things that make *you* who you are. The things that have shaped you, the things that influence your perspective, establish your values, and keep you going forward. Sometimes you have to take a long, hard look in the mirror. It is imperative that you learn how to assess your own behavior and recognize that maybe you are the one who must shift, grow, mature, change, and stop blaming others.

Self-care is taking your power back. Self-care includes holding yourself accountable to make changes when you need to. Most often, the heart work is the hardest work of all.

It's super easy to get lost in the manis and pedis, the bubble baths, the candles, and glorious moments of enjoying a nice glass of red, but we have to get down and dirty with ourselves.

Inner peace looks good on you.

Self-care is all about self—no exception. All of who we are. Physical, mental, emotional, financial, sexual, and, first and foremost, spiritual.

Self-care starts with self-forgiveness, as I mentioned earlier.

You are a divine feminine goddess. Act accordingly.

The number one lie we cling to for dear life is that we aren't a good person because …

Fill in the blank with whatever you keep telling yourself. It could be something from twenty years ago, or it could be the guilt you feel for yelling at your kids last night. Whatever it is, you deserve to release it.

Forgiving yourself opens the door to endless possibilities. Possibilities of hope, of change, and of course for growth. Forgiveness starts within; it's an inside job. When you can work through all the hurt, pain, guilt, and shame you have been carrying around with you, then and only then have you truly committed to your self-care journey at the level you deserve. Nourish your mind, body, and soul in ways that fuel you, all while setting new boundaries of what you no longer will tolerate or accept in your life from others and, more importantly, from yourself. Release anything that is pulling you down. Say no to requests for your time that don't align. Take charge and full responsibility for your life. That is what self-care is all about. Rearrange your life with health at the center of it and experience the rewards in ways you've never imagined. Clear you circle of distractors; people who discourage you from being bold, being seen and heard, and being you. They don't belong there.

A very wise woman once told me that it hurts less to forgive immediately than to harbor resentment toward someone who did you wrong. That wise woman was my beautiful grandmother. She is a diehard Baptist woman through and through. She is one of the well-behaved women who raised me. Although she did ease up in her seventies and beyond, her message was clear. Hanging on to hurt or counting wrongs leads to very toxic relationships and negative thoughts about the person you feel upset with, yet it only eats away at you. Why this is so valuable to me, and why I share it with you now, is because Grammamere was and is the happiest woman I have ever met or known. Unfortunately, dementia took my beautiful grandmother from me many years ago but to this day she still has a smile on her face. There must be a reason!

Forgiving others doesn't excuse them of their responsibility, but it does free you of the attachment to them. Don't underestimate the turmoil that unresolved emotional baggage can cause in your life. When you keep the door open to old wounds, you cut off your ability to fully heal and move forward. You cut off your ability to receive greatness. You deserve better than that. New doors hold new opportunities. Close the doors you must close and be ready for new doors to open.

A Prayer for Guidance

Dear God, I am so caught up in all kinds of things from my past. I worry about choices I have made and people I have hurt. I am angry at people who have hurt me. Help me to release the heartache and anger. Show me how to love myself unconditionally and to start building my life in a healthier way. I desire freedom from hurt, and I want to explore what is possible for me. Thank you for keeping me safe all these years and for loving me even when I have not loved myself. I am on the edge of change, and I am ready to respect myself and make better choices for my life. Amen.

CHAPTER 19

Confession: I Stopped Hitting Snooze on My Life

Have you ever felt like you were sleeping on your dreams? Do you catch yourself saying, "One day …"? The most self-sabotaging pattern women get into is saying, "One day, when the kids are raised," or "One day, when I have the money," or "One day, when I have more time, I'll do x, y, z." Then, one day never comes!

I made a decision a long time ago that my dreams are important.

They matter, and they are possible! Just because someone else doesn't believe in or pursue their dreams doesn't mean I can't.

I stopped hitting snooze on my ideas and started waking up with purpose. Purpose attracts possibilities! I believe this and know it to be true.

Every single morning starts the same. I'm a creature of habit. As a commitment to my higher self and ultimately becoming my best self, I start each morning in prayer, throw on my workout clothes, drink some water, then coffee, read a personal development or wealth-consciousness book, and then I journal. Once I feel ready to work out, I get it in and then shower, and then I'm ready for an incredible day! I do this every single day because it sets me up for success. Successful people exercise their minds and their bodies.

I've been doing this routine for so many years it's automatic now. It's a non-negotiable part of my day and is the most significant self-care ritual I have created. Starting my morning right creates the vibe I want to carry with me all day. If you still haven't implemented a personal development practice, you are missing out. I know so many people who thought it wasn't for them; they were living well. Once they started reading, journaling, and building their mindset, they couldn't imagine not having had started. I think that's one of the biggest myths out there – that personal development is for unhappy people. No, quite the opposite, actually. Start today and never look back. It will take some new habit formation but is so worth it. You are worth it, and so are your dreams, whatever they are!

It feels so long ago, like another lifetime ago, but the old me would get up early—I've always been an early riser—but I'd chug along. I didn't necessarily have a routine, but I also didn't know about the power in personal development either. I didn't drink coffee back in the day, so I'd stuff down something unhealthy, toast or a bagel, and I definitely didn't work out, so exercise wasn't happening, and…well, let's just say I needed a change. Big-time. Can you relate to that feeling? Knowing that you must make a change because staying the same is no longer an option? The title of this chapter is all about a self-care practice I implemented not just in my morning routine but in all activities. I stopped chugging along and got intentional about my life.

Mornings set the tone for the day, and, therefore, it's super important you get your morning routine sorted out. I stopped waiting for the right time to change. I gave up all my excuses and created it myself, and I encourage you to do the same. I activate my ability to think more clearly and to receive when I stay consistent in my morning routine. It sets the tone for the day, yes, but also, for my success in the long-game. I won't tell you to get up at five o'clock in the morning like some other self-help dudes, but if that's your desire, go for it. The routine is up to you. The benefits will amaze you, particularly if you currently run around frazzled in the mornings. Think about it. If that's how you start each day, no wonder things feel out of alignment. How could you show up as your badass self if you're functioning on caffeine and chaos? You can't. Stop trying to make it work because it won't. Lock in an aligned routine and become unstoppable. You will feel a shift energetically after the first day. Every time you make a promise to yourself and follow through on it, you are building your confidence. It's a win-win situation. You can make it happen. Look at your current schedule. What is working and what's wasted time? Want to listen to a podcast or an audiobook? Hop on the treadmill or exercise bike and get to it, girl!

Hitting snooze on my life was more about being stuck in hesitation versus doing things. It looked like this: not finishing my next book because I wanted the best publishing deal, not recording training videos for my programs because I wanted the best background setup and the perfect lighting to do it in, or not pitching myself to certain TV shows because I wanted to lose twenty pounds first. Yes, those are real-life examples from yours truly, and let's just say I had to recognize and own the fact that they were all just excuses. They were my made-up stories of why I couldn't do all the things I really wanted to do. They were the excuses I kept playing over in my head in order to protect myself from failure and also from taking action. I had to call myself out. Calling yourself out on your negative behavior is self-care at its finest. You cannot be committed to living your best life and fighting for your excuses at the same time. You've got to hold yourself accountable and tune into your patterns that rely on fear to thrive.

Once you're aware of them, you can't keep protecting them. They are what they are, and they're causing you to miss out on some great pleasure and success.

I finished my book (you're reading it right now). I recorded a bunch of videos. I pitched myself for my own show and *got it*. I started recording my own TV show, *Women Who Lead*, and rocked it! If you are procrastinating on doing some great things in your life, this is your wake-up call. Stop hitting snooze and get up and go for it. You are in charge of your life, and the results you are getting are all a direct reflection of your effort. If you start thinking of your dreams as non-negotiables and trust that everything you desire desires you, it will give you momentum. You are good enough to have what you want right now. You can make changes to your health and your body along the way. Do not hold yourself back out of fear. If you need a confidence boost, follow through on your promises to yourself. Hold yourself accountable and transform your life. It's one of the best ways to continuously build your confidence muscle. Stop breaking promises to yourself. Who was it? Someone said, "Done is better than perfect." They were on to something there. It's true, albeit, I don't care for the saying per se. When we sit around waiting for God to give us the sign we prayed for, or for the weather to be perfect, or the client to show up, we are wasting precious time and energy.

Pray, trust, act. Those three words have made a huge difference in my life, and I know they can in yours too. Stop worrying about how things will work out and start taking action. Claim your future by stepping up and taking action on your goals. Close your eyes and visualize your ideal day in the life of next-level you. What does it look like? When do you wake up? Are you well rested or tired? What's your morning ritual? How do you feel?

Repeat this as often as necessary until the visualization becomes your new normal. That's how it's done. You decide and take action. If you've really had enough of playing life at your current level, then you will choose to do something about it. Only you can make it happen. Stop living on autopilot and start living in the moment. Time is a gift. Do not waste it.

When we break down why most people hit snooze on their alarm clocks, it's because they aren't getting enough sleep. Period. What happens though is the people constantly hitting snooze are disrupting their sleep even more. Just as a doctor would recommend you go to bed earlier and establish a nighttime routine, so will you benefit if you establish a morning routine. Apply that basic strategy to every single goal you have, and you'll be creating more success for yourself, achieving your goals, and feeling better. If you have given up your own goals in the face of exhaustion or some other reason, get back in the game. Figure out what you want to do to feel better. Maybe that goal is getting an extra hour of sleep each night, or drinking less wine, or exercising for thirty minutes three days a week. Maybe, it's a complete overhaul of your life? Whatever it is, commit to it. Think of every goal you have for yourself right now and visualize the end result you want. Then picture yourself hitting snooze on it each time you think of it. Weird, right? Why visualize your desired outcome and then choose to continuously hit snooze on it? That's what you're doing when you say things like, "Oh, I'll start tomorrow," or "I need to release this excess weight first," or "What if nobody buys my book or program," or whatever story you are making up about your specific goals and why it's not the right timing or you're not the right person. You are way too smart to be shortchanging yourself. Focus on creating your secretly fantasized-about dream life and stop fueling your fears and excuses. No more hitting snooze on your life. You won't find the inspiration you're looking for inside your current routine. Shake it up, sis. Do something different. Watch the energy around you and inside you shift. See yourself blossoming into the powerhouse you were born to be and stop the cycle you're in. If you need an accountability coach, hire one. Get going. You've waited long enough. Believe that there is so much more available for you because there is.

Note: If you are tired and on the verge of exhaustion and really feel like you can't muster up the energy to do one more thing, go to your health specialist immediately and get blood work done. That's the best way to see if there's something physical going on. Hormones and sleep need each other to function at their optimal levels, so if you need to, make an appointment for your wellness checkup right now.

Taking the best care of your mind and body is how you're going to live your best life.

A Prayer for Guidance

Dear God, help me to feel energized about my goals. I want to live life to its fullest. I'm so tired and feel lost at times. Help me to find clarity and to commit to my own success. I know that my dreams matter, and I want to make them come true. I believe in myself but need some extra energy. Take my worries and fears and allow me to start trusting that I was made for something more. Allow me to trust in you. Amen.

CHAPTER 20

Confession: I Am Not a Yes Woman

Hands up if you've ever said yes to somebody out of a sense of obligation and not a true desire to do the damn thing. Whoa! Yes, I'm going there. I'm being so honest right now I'm feeling a teeny bit nauseous as I type this out. I can just imagine some of my past acquaintances sitting there scratching their head and wondering if they were one of those people. For the sake of argument, yeah, probably at one time or another. Yeah, you were, but I take responsibility for it all, so, moving along. It is what it is, and that's all that it is, and I know I'm not the only woman in the world who has agreed to do things that she did not necessarily want to do or felt resentful toward. This includes but is not limited to spouses, children, siblings, parents, in-laws, friends, co-workers, clients, and neighbors. I mean, some of you want to be invited to things that you know you'll never attend.

Diving into this chapter feels so necessary because there are women all over the world doing things that they don't want to do for the sake of not being judged or called rude or selfish, or mom-shamed, or labeled whatever fill-in-the-blank people are using nowadays. I talked about this during my recent radio interview on *What She Said Talk Radio*. You can listen to it on YouTube. Every time a woman says sorry for something that does not merit an apology; she depletes her self-esteem. Same goes for every yes, a woman says out of obligation. When you do things that are out of alignment for you, it will only hurt you. It also teaches you not to trust yourself. There is still such a different standard for men, and I refuse to continue accepting that as normal. What I mean by that, in case I lost you there, is that men say no all the time to joining charity boards, volunteering to fold church bulletins, or bake two dozen cupcakes for their child's school fundraiser, and guess what? Nobody questions it or gossips about them for declining. Guess what else? Men will say no without any justification, and it's accepted. Men don't fumble to form some sort of an apology; they say no and they mean it. Period. They use that old adage, n-o spells no. Boom! Done! No justification. Just two letters.

Women! We are definitely a different breed. Some of you will still be apologizing a month later for not being able to help out at an event for reasons that don't even make sense. We lose sleep over saying no. We feel guilty at times for saying no. We can get ourselves twisted up into knots over saying no. We waste time worrying about saying no. Stop it, ladies! The easiest and most efficient solution is to let your yes be yes and your no be no. Period.

For many years, I was afraid of letting people down. It tied into figuring out that I was worthy whether I helped people or not, and if I did what they wanted or expected of me or not. Believe me, a lot of choices I made many years ago in relation to friendships and dating were directly linked to my fear of being abandoned, rejected, or not needed if I had the audacity to say no to them. Same theory can be applied to many late work nights where I left my family to do public education for an organization I was working at and received no thanks, ever. I literally put my work first because that's what good women do when they work outside of the home. Right? All of those extra hours and late nights got me nowhere. I have clearly evolved since those days, but at the time, I was worried about disappointing an ungrateful boss more than my family. That is so messed up, and I know some of you are going through that right now.

Saying no is not evil, and it certainly doesn't make me selfish, and it doesn't make you any of those things either. Isn't it interesting how someone will call you selfish for putting your needs first yet, they want you to put their needs above yours? See the irony there?

I actually do enjoy helping people! That's why I've worked in the social services sector for two decades. I also believe firmly that doing things for others for any reason other than you truly wanting to is not healthy. In fact, it's a disservice to yourself and the involved individual. When I was busy doing all the things for other people, I wasn't happy. How could I have been? I was exhausted and underappreciated, and I was doing it to myself! As a result of over giving and overdoing for everyone else, I started flaking out in my friendships. I was tired. I volunteered as a director and active member for four different boards, networks, and committees at one point, all while running my own company, raising my son, and being that wife that packed my husband's lunch, with a little love note to boot! Although my household still ran smoothly and I was on my game for all the things, I was more irritable at times than I would like to have been. The thought of hosting a couples' night in was enough to keep me wrapped up in my duvet, not wanting to answer the phone. I love hosting get-togethers with friends and pride myself on my charcuterie board skills, but in those days, I resented having to do the prep work and entertain people out of sheer obligation—because they expected it, and I didn't want to disappoint them. Totally on me! My husband wasn't tired. He enjoyed having friends over. He would go to work each day Monday through Friday, golf when he wanted, and come home to fancy meals prepared and ready to eat when he walked in the door, his lunch packed. He didn't see my frustration when friends didn't know when it was time to leave. Party's over, folks! Bye! But I digress. Instead of resenting him and being upset, I started asking for help with meals and stopped trying to do everything myself. I had to. I was ready to explode! How many of you are still pretending that you're okay with doing everything and running a business or managing a career on top of it all? Can you say on the verge of burnout? Ladies, stop giving to other people before you give to yourself and your loved ones. Make it mandatory for yourself to take care of your needs first before anyone else, and that includes your partner and children. You've heard it one million times, but you cannot pour anything from an empty cup. Fill your cup; your red Solo cup counts too.

The thing is I kind of sort of get why it's not always easy to outright just say no. I was raised to help others whenever possible. My parents were both big on volunteering within the small community I grew up in, and as a member of Girl Guides for twelve-plus years, it was my duty to help whenever possible. I won't even entertain sharing the good ole Baptist girl guilt I used to feel when I started saying no to people.

So, how do you go from one extreme of always saying yes to the opposite, saying no? You pick your hard! You look out for numero uno. What feels better? Overextending yourself and keeping a crazy schedule to be available to help others all the time or truly only saying yes when it is convenient for you and you actually want to do the thing? The choice is yours and yours alone. If you give yourself permission to set limits and implement boundaries on your time, you will inevitably feel better. If you overextend yourself and do things you don't want to do, you will feel drained, resentful, and most likely tired. Choose wisely, gorgeous.

Setting boundaries for yourself means you stop stretching yourself so thin that when you say yes, you can show up eager and energized to help.

I'd say yes to people who I had no intention of hanging out with because it was easier in the moment, but then when I would bail on them, it felt out of alignment for the woman I wanted to be. Very unqueenly behavior. When the dinner date came around, I wanted to snuggle up on my couch under my big, fluffy blanket and watch a Hallmark movie. No way did I want to get dressed up and splurge on a dinner over superficial conversation. Especially, those dinners that I was expected to foot the bill. So, I evaluated the friendships that were important to me and healthy for me at that stage in my life, and I started saying no when invited to anything that wasn't a fit. That's how I roll these days, too. Intentional AF! It's not your responsibility to do things with people you have outgrown or with whom you no longer vibe. Too many women keep friends around because they grew up together or because they feel rude cutting them off. When you look at it from a growth perspective and take ownership of your inner circle, you can see how important it is to be surrounded by aligned friends—people who lift you up, support you, and you grow with.

This didn't happen overnight for me, and it most likely won't for you either, but start assessing your circle and calendar. Who are you giving your energy and time to? Evaluate your list and go from there. You start by changing your patterns of behavior one action at a time. Saying no without an explanation will feel weird at first for some of you, especially if you are the one who is always saying yes because people have come to expect a yes from you, but don't let that stop you.

I created non-negotiable policies and boundaries for myself, which included blocked-off *me* time in my calendar, and I encourage you to do the same. What are you available for and what are you not available for? How do you want to feel when you say yes to helping others? Certain, excited, confident, mentally focused? Those are some ideas. Sort through your own idea of what a yes means to you and don't apologize for it to anyone.

As a wild thinker and creative person who falls under the umbrella of both an entrepreneur and lady boss, I tend to see the world very differently from others who don't live in my kind of world. I can appreciate the lens of an employee, as I worked for others for most of my career history. However, I was born to lead, born to speak up, and called to impact millions and millions of people all around the world. I needed to break out from the nine-to-five mentality, the desperation for a vacation, or living for the weekend. The "ideal" life of working through the week and getting blitzed all weekend to pretend you're satisfied with your life has never appealed to me. I felt sick when surrounded by people who thought the biggest success in life was to make $45,000 a year, own a car, and spend your weekends with former high school friends (not judging, just saying), hitting up bars, reminiscing about the good old days while watching your husband play beer pong. This will rub some women the wrong way because, well, some of you say you are happy with that kind of lifestyle. Are you really though? Or do you not understand that there's more pleasure and new adventures waiting for you to say yes? Evolving as a woman leads to experiencing more joy and pleasure in your life. It includes figuring out who you are and what you really want out of your time here on earth. You don't have to pretend to be satisfied with anything. You also don't have to pretend to be the same person you were years ago. I work with a lot of women who say they feel stuck because they don't want to leave their marriage but there's no passion, no connection with their partner anymore because they've outgrown them. This happens due to lack of communication, mostly, and the fact that not everyone understands the value in evolution.

One of my personal policies is this: if you are not fully satisfied in your relationships or career, do not approach me to tell me which dreams of mine are too big or too small. We don't play the same game in life and we certainly don't speak the same language.

Here's the thing. A lot of people are doing things they don't like to do and then wondering why their faith remains in question most of the time, or why their marriages, parenting, and friendships are all falling apart or not going as well as they want them to. Your attitude matters! What you do with your energy and time matters. Do you know how many women will go to their grave resentful, unhappy, and wanting so much more in their lives? Do you know why?

I'll enlighten you. Women who live on the sidelines, always putting others first, live on empty; therefore, they cannot focus on their own dreams and their own wants. Even the sweetest woman in the world is going to feel resentful toward the people she feels abuse her time or energy. It's not rocket science. You need to make a choice right now. What kind of woman do you want to be? Start doing the things that woman does and stop doing the things that woman would not do.

You are not alive to pay your bills, make little Billy a sandwich, and die. Your sole purpose in life is not to raise your children and sacrifice your own dreams. What happens when the children leave home and you're left empty and confused about who you are? Or even worse! What happens if your son or daughter don't pursue their dreams and settle for a mediocre life? Sis, it's your choice to make. You can get intentional about your health, your goals, and your relationships—or not. It is completely up to you. It doesn't have to be as complicated as you can make it feel.

Evaluation time. How satisfied are you with your life right now?

On a scale of one to ten, ten being completely satisfied, one being completely unsatisfied, where are you sitting?

1 2 3 4 5 6 7 8 9 10

What is the first step to becoming more satisfied with your life? Think about it but don't overthink it. One small shift can change a lot if you commit to following through. Turn the dial one notch at a time.

You will experience a boost in your confidence and self-esteem when you start being true to yourself and your values. God did not create you to be a yes woman. You have much more purpose than giving to the point of feeling depleted. Remember when you were young and you had all kinds of ideas about what you wanted to do? Think back to those ideas and ask yourself, What changed? What got in the way of you pursuing them? If you put your time and energy into creating your best life and made time to help others when you wanted to, what would change for you?

Say it with me: "I am no longer holding onto people who need to exit my life."

It's time to allow what needs to go to be released. Don't hang on to people or commitments that no longer serve a purpose in your life. When someone loves you or respects you, they want the best for you and will understand that you have limits on your time. Whatever relationships need to end will end. Maybe there's a friend you have disconnected with lately who is feeling like she has outgrown you but is too afraid to address it with you. What about the other woman waiting in line to sit on the board that's taking up your Monday evenings as a new director, or the woman waiting to organize the school fundraiser that you keep saying yes to out of obligation or fear of being judged if you say no? You may be taking up space and opportunities for other women who are excited to get started. Think about each commitment you have made out of fear of disappointing someone. Pray about it. It's time to reorganize your calendar and create your life by intention. Don't overthink it because you already know what feels good and what feels heavy. This is a new chapter for you, one where you step into your fierce feminine power and take control of your schedule in a way you never have before.

Let your yes be yes and your no be no.

A Prayer for Guidance

Dear God, I see how my busy calendar is a reflection of me feeling needed. I acknowledge that I have been filling up space in order to avoid working on myself. I am ready to have more time to spend on my own dreams and to be with my family. I want to be confident in saying yes only when I want to. I need some extra support and guidance right now as I evaluate my commitments and relationships. Help me decipher which ones to keep and which ones to let go of. Amen.

POWER THOUGHTS FOR EMOTIONAL STABILITY

I love and accept myself as I am.

I am competent and capable.

I am worthy of inner peace.

I am in control of my emotions.

I am building healthy relationships.

I am safe and loved.

I adapt to change with ease.

I set healthy boundaries that create healthy relationships.

I am courageous and stand up for myself.

I am confident in my decision-making skills.

I am free from my past and live in the now.

I acknowledge my emotions without attachment.

I attract experiences that serve my highest good.

It is safe for me to be honest about my feelings.

I am ready to release what no longer serves me and embrace my next chapter.

I am abundantly blessed with supportive relationships.

FINANCIAL HEALTH SELF-CARE

CHAPTER 21

Confession: I Accepted that Debt Is Not a Dirty Word

How many times have you ignored your gut instinct only to regret it later?

C'mon, hands up! I see you, sis! Let's have a moment of silence and release the regret, guilt, and doubt you've been carrying around with you about all the things you have done or purchased on impulse against your better judgment. Owning your choices and releasing any low vibes still lingering around long after their expiration date allows you to free up space to get clear on how to tune into your intuition to make healthier decisions. The ability to tune in and listen to that inner voice, whose sole purpose is to be your safeguard, will change your life if you let it. It's available to you free of charge. No interest! All you need to do is pause, take a few deep breaths, and release whatever tension you feel. A lot of women I work with ask me how to know when their intuition is trying to guide them.

Intuition is your inner voice, a gut reaction, or an instant feeling you get about something or someone. Too many women don't trust themselves because they have made poor choices in the past. We all have. I will guarantee that when you listen to your intuition, things always work out. The best way I have described the sensation to my clients is this: intuition is a feeling in your body. The usual feeling people report is associated with anxious and fearful thoughts; that is fear. Thoughts are different from feelings, but thoughts cause feelings. Fear lives in your mind and is usually loud and more recognizable because fear consumes so many women. The art of learning how to tap into your intuition is in the practice of actually listening—being still and sorting through immediate sensations. If it feels light, it's your intuition; if it feels dark or heavy, that is usually fear. Unless you are in immediate danger, to which fear would be an appropriate response. Did I confuse you yet?

Think about a relationship, a job offer, or a purchase you made that at the time felt off or perhaps not 100 percent the right idea, but you went ahead and did the thing anyway because you didn't want to lose out on the date, the pay raise, or the shoe flash sale. Then as things progressed, you started to *feel* like you had made the wrong decision. Take it up a notch, and think about a time when you went out shopping. Let's call it retail therapy. You went out and spent a load of money on clothing that you still haven't worn or doesn't quite fit right, or the shoes you thought you could cram your feet into hurt too much. All of those purchases felt good at the time but were not in your best interest, and now you're trying to figure out how you'll pay the minimum payment on your credit card.

I know the feeling all too well. I have made large investments in my education, business coaching and masterminds, and DIY programs to grow my business (still waiting to be opened on my laptop). Some of the purchases were *hell yes* transactions, and some were not. Needless to say, I've learned a lot of expensive lessons. There's nothing worse than begrudgingly having to pay that credit card bill or mentor every month. It's an entirely different experience and energy when you are eager to pay.

Do you feel like you'll never be free of your debt?

Do you lose sleep worrying about how you will pay your bills?

Is money the reason you say no to things you want to say yes to?

Do you believe in your ability to live financially free?

When I got to work on healing my money story, I uncovered a lot of BS thoughts and beliefs that were hindering my ability to make more money and feeding my debt collection.

Here are a few of my old stories and beliefs that may resonate with you:

- I didn't come from money.
- It was selfish to want to have a lot of money.

- Where I came from, people didn't have a lot of money.
- As soon as I get money, it's gone.
- Making a lot of money was hard for someone like me.
- Debt was a part of life; a constant struggle I'd never escape.

Throughout the process of tearing up my money beliefs and planting new ones, I hired mentors, read numerous books, and listened to every Abraham Hicks YouTube video I could find. I highly recommend the money rampages. They are so good. So uplifting.

The moment I decided that it was safe for me to make money was the same moment I committed to living free of money pain or shame. I spent so much time locked in a financial lack mentality. Now, I don't even allow conversations of lack to occur in my space, by anyone.

I teach my clients how to release the financial burdens they've been carrying for years and learn how to build a healthy relationship with money. I want every woman to be financially fit AF. I know what shifts when you release the chaos around money and tap into your feminine power to receive. It's called expansion. I know the difference in feeling ashamed of debt and the liberating experience in feeling neutral about it. When you change your mindset around money, you change your ability to receive it. You have to take radical responsibility for your financial goals, current situation, and dreams without apologizing. You won't be able to attract the abundance you desire when you feel ashamed of desiring it in the first place. You will only attract more of the same. If it's more debt, that's what will show up for you. Think about it. What is your current money vibe? Do you give money a purpose? Have you accepted your money desires, or do you still feel greedy or selfish for wanting money? It is safe for you to receive. I believe that good women do good things with money. Stop pretending you don't want money, and to my lady bosses, stop starting every sentence about your business with "It's not about the money," because honestly, the longer you speak that nonsense, the longer you will struggle. When you create a business doing what you love to help others and to have a greater impact in the world, you deserve to be well compensated beyond your wildest dreams. Own it. Declare it. Trust it. To be clear, that applies to all of you stay-at-home moms, women working for someone else, and all of you womanpreneurs trying to figure this out.

You get to fully decide what role money will play in your life. Money is a resource. It will flow into your life with ease if you let it. You don't have to identify with your current debt or sabotage yourself around your receiving potential. Today, in this moment, you get to release the baggage you've been carrying around and start fresh. No, your debt won't magically disappear, although anything is possible.

In times when I was down on my knees, scared, and begging God through tears of shame and fear, I promised to help as many women as possible if I could finally, once and for all, make amends with money and my desire for wanting a lot of it. This book along with my other books and my coaching services are me fulfilling that promise. Healing my money story has allowed me to create a beautiful life, continue to pay off debt, share my heart and soul teachings with women all over the world, and show my son that anything is possible. I am currently debt-free at forty! Figuring out how to use self-care rituals alongside the law of attraction has completely upgraded my life, and I want that for you too.

Money is energy, and I can assure you that functioning from a place of fear-based financial decisions is no way to receive more. Feeling broke, struggling to pay your bills, or figuring out what bill you'll have to skip this month is not going to feel good, and when you don't feel good, you attract more things to not feel good about—and vice versa. Whatever you tell yourself about money is how it will exist in your life. I've been working on my money mindset and wealth consciousness for nearly a decade, and I continue to. It's not a one and done. If you are ready to live differently, make the decision and get started now.

I hold a firm belief that I am not responsible for anyone's money story, and it is not my job to convince someone of my worth. That, in and of itself, has completely overhauled my ability to let money flow to me in expected and unexpected ways. I teach my clients that someone choosing not to buy from them or hire them because it's too expensive isn't about the client – it's the buyer's perception of value and most likely, a low-vibe money mindset and lack of belief in themselves. Your peace of mind is always available to you, for free, any time, any day, anywhere. It's your responsibility to work on obtaining and sustaining inner peace. Nobody can do that for you. Nobody knows what soothes your soul and mind better than you. Financial stress will eat you up and spit you out if you let it.

At some point in my journey, I made the decision that debt is neither good nor bad; it just is what it is. Some things I pay with cash up front, and other things I put on a credit card and pay accordingly. Great! Makes sense. Sounds easy enough. It wasn't—until I allowed it to be. I was so locked into thinking I was my debt instead of separating who I am with owing money. I felt so dirty and lived in embarrassment about different financial decisions I had made that it was consuming me. Do you know how difficult it is to attract money when you're throwing yourself a pity party about how horrible you are at managing it? First, I made the decision to not identify with my debt. Second, I acknowledged that many of the reasons I had accumulated debt started when I was a single mother, working three jobs, earning my postsecondary education, solely responsible for another human and had no clue about managing or attracting money. All I knew was struggle. Acknowledging that helped relieve some of the internal pressure. I was not willy-nilly in my financial decisions. I was busting my ass to do the best I could, and putting it in perspective like that allowed me to see that I did what I had to do. When is the last time you put your money situation into perspective?

Women often neglect to acknowledge that self-care includes financial wellness. One of the best ways to overcome financial struggles is to get to know your money. What is your income? What are your bank balances, credit card balances, and outgoing financial responsibilities? Take inventory and get it sorted. Do not be afraid to face your money. The sooner you address your financial skeletons, the sooner you can start to heal your money story and commit to making better decisions. You are not your debt, and debt is not a *dirty* word.

The next best thing you can do is come to terms with how you currently feel about money.

If you're like me, you grew up with money never being talked about except for the "money doesn't grow on trees" and "wait until payday" kinds of conversations. Ugh! Shout out to all the parents who were trying to do their best. I have chosen a totally different money story and dialogue to raise my son with. I talk about money with my son, and I always have, at age-appropriate levels. My son will never know the struggles I carried and challenges I faced as a single mother for his first four years, nor does he need to. He was always cared for, and I always made money, so he never went without anything. My husband accepted full responsibility to support us in the ways he could when we got married, and I maintained financial responsibility for my son. Look at us now, Mr. Primetime! And we're only getting started! It's primetime to shine!

Do you have a secret spending habit? Do you feel guilty when you spend money on yourself? Do you fear looking at your debt on paper? Are you avoiding answering every unknown number because you fear it is another debt collector?

Release those negative feelings and thoughts and intentionally focus on improving your connection with yourself and with God. How you feel about yourself will tell me a lot about how you feel about money. The best advice I ever received was to use prayer as a request for a solution to a problem and then meditate to hear the answer. When I started praying about my financial situation and asking for guidance to live a more abundant life, the answers were delivered. I had to get intentional about receiving support with sorting out my money, and I forgave myself for making decisions that were based on a lack mindset. I also forgave myself for spending money on things trying to impress people who didn't care. Then I did the necessary work to change. I started having conversations with my husband about our money and our lifestyle. We, together, sorted through what we were not willing to give up and what we were willing to do to release the debt and live even better. We are well on our way. God is good!

Get intentional about clearing up your money situation. Hire a financial advisor and start paying that lingering debt that's accumulating interest like bees to honey. Let go of the shame and fear that's robbing you of joy.

Your other job is to turn up the d*mn volume and stop resisting what your intuition is trying to tell you. Developing a relationship with your inner being will completely change your life and your finances. You deserve to experience prosperity. God wants you to live an abundant life. You deserve to live free of financial pain. There is so much money on the other side of shame waiting for you. Decide you get to have it all. Commit to cleaning up your money energy and create a new story. That's all it takes. Then do the work. Shift your vibe and let it be fun and easy. I know it sounds crazy to you right now because you are so caught up in your debt and money pain, and cannot see what's possible. Everything changes when you are no longer available for less than what you desire. Turn up the volume. Raise your vibration. It's time to tell a different money story and experience the abundance God desires for your life.

A Prayer for Guidance

Dear God, I am so stressed out about money. I worry about not having any, and when I do get some, I have to pay it out. It feels scary for me to trust that money can flow into my life easily. Help me to heal my money story. I want to release the struggle and the shame I feel. Help me to feel worthy of receiving money, more money than I have ever imagined. I want to live better. The more money I make, the more people I can help. I am ready to tell a different story and live in abundance and limitless blessings. Help me to radically shift my money beliefs. Amen.

CHAPTER 22

Confession: I Stopped Apologizing

To everyone. For everything. Most significantly, to myself.

In plain and simple English, I stopped saying sorry when I wasn't. Let me tell you, from my lips to God's ears, it completely changed my life and my bank account. Saying sorry for your dreams, saying sorry for your money goals, saying sorry for wanting more than your friends is holding you back from having everything your heart desires. I love talking about this for many reasons but mostly, as I mentioned earlier in the book, every time a woman says sorry without merit her self-esteem goes down, down, down.

I have been addressing this with family, friends, and clients for many years. Google my interview on *What She Said Talk Radio*. I'm serious! It's a short video that explains more about this topic.

Many women live their lives apologizing for existing, apologizing for wanting careers outside of the home or for wanting to run businesses online while they travel, apologizing for saying no, for not wanting six kids and a minivan, and apologizing for dreaming bigger than people around them. Who knew that constantly saying sorry was eating away at you on an emotional level? If you are a chronic apologizer, it's time to change your ways. There is nothing to apologize for. You are uniquely you. God has given you a vision for your life that nobody sees but you. You can try to share it with others and convince them you're not crazy, or you can actively work on bringing your vision to life.

I stopped compromising my desires, my values, and my beliefs for others. I made a decision. I decided I was no longer available for drama. I decided I would no longer try to impress people who clearly didn't care in the first place. I decided I was going to unleash my inner badass and be true to myself no matter who thought I was being too bold. I decided I was going to stop apologizing for loving my body just because it made women who didn't love theirs feel uncomfortable. I decided it was safe for me to have everything I always wanted without justifying why I deserved it. Every single area of my life needed an overhaul, and my finances were no exception. Sigh! Such liberating decisions. Have you noticed a pattern yet? Decide. Commit. Act. In everything you desire and need to change in your life, it all starts with a decision.

I stopped saying sorry for working on my dreams, taking time to write, taking time to get a massage, to get my lashes done, or my hair done. I also stopped saying yes to appease other people. Saying no as a complete sentence is powerful. I've been teaching women how to do that for more than a decade, and I have written about the power of no in two of my books. Remember that saying from when you were a little girl, n-o spells no! Why did we ever stop using it so confidently? We used to shout it out so everyone could hear us. What happened to that powerful little girl? Did she grow up to be a subdued woman?

We are inundated with quotes, books, and T-shirts with the saying *love yourself*. So, why then are women made to feel some sort of shady guilt for actually doing so? It's not healthy to go through life feeling inferior or insecure about who you are or what you look like. It wastes so much precious time and energy. We are all deserving of love, and it has to start within ourselves.

You have to stop letting other people's words fill your mind with doubt and worry. Your job is to focus on your attitude and your mood. You get to choose how you think and how you feel. You get to ask for what you want and not back it up with a reason of why you're worthy to have it. Remind yourself as often as necessary that you are worthy of everything you want because you are. Period. No explanation needed. You get to take a stand for your dreams without feeling weird about it. You get to distract yourself from other people's opinions. Have you ever told anyone about your dreams or lofty desires? What was their reaction? How did their reaction impact you?

A lot of the negativity I had to clear out of my head wasn't coming from me at all. It was coming from people who didn't want me to outshine them. People who felt so strongly that I should just be happy with what I had. They thought I was selfish to want more and to actually go after it. That is on them; it's not my issue. I am thankful for all that I have and I want more. Deal with it.

I am open to loved ones' honest feelings about me and my impact on their lives so long as it is coming from a pure-hearted place and not jealousy. But when someone tells me I must change before I am allowed to feel good enough, I walk away. No, I run away.

I essentially stepped up to the plate and went full swing into living my best life, even though that meant some people dropped off the face of my world. The people who matter most to me have been and continue to be my biggest cheerleaders. My husband admires my tenacity. He says I inspire him to think bigger and to believe in the unbelievable. My son watches me continue to soar and believes anything is possible for him too. If I had given into the fears and the doubts, how would my son believe that? He wouldn't. He would think that playing small is normal and that living an average life is safer than chasing after your dreams. No thank you! After reading chapter 8, you understand more clearly why I had to go big or stay home. Our children are watching our every move. What are you teaching yours?

You see, when you take ownership of your life, and you start to improve your confidence and body image, some people will become jealous or uncomfortable. It's like women are accustomed to griping and complaining about their bodies, their husbands, and their secret shopping habits, and when a woman doesn't, she is outcasted or called conceited. When you put in the effort—the blood, sweat, and tears—to become healthier, it either inspires those around you or it makes them feel uncomfortable because they are okay with mediocre. I remember a time when I was very strict about my diet. I was committed to releasing excess weight and was eating fairly clean—mostly green veggies and meat, and I would specify how I wanted my veggies sautéed or my meat cooked when ordering at a restaurant. This one time in particular, my girlfriends and I were having a blast and enjoying some good red wine when it came time to order. Most of my friends were eating similarly, but there was one who mocked me and insisted I was being too picky about my food. Let's just say she knew in her heart that she, too, needed to eat better, but because she wasn't ready to, she felt triggered by my commitment to myself.

Does that happen to you? It could be applicable to anything you are doing to change your life. Maybe you're going to the gym early in the morning, and your friend thinks you're crazy to get up at six and go because she is not as disciplined or committed to results as you are. Or how about spending more nights at home because you're saving money for a new car, and your friend feels guilty that she can't set a goal and follow through on it. Money talk is no different. There is the type of woman who empowers fellow women to think bigger, raise their rates, and set big money goals, and then there are women who act weird about money—the women who gossip about the women living larger, talking about money, and teaching about manifesting a lot of money. See the difference? Which type of woman are you? Do you feel triggered by a woman who believes in herself and pursues her passion and monetizes it? Are you intimidated by the woman who asks for what she wants and needs in a friendship? In a team meeting? Or at the restaurant? Check in with what your behavior pattern is. You'll never feel your best if, instead of changing your life, you sit in comparison and judge others.

When I stopped watching other women and how they ran their online business, things got better for me. I started tapping into desire, to soul and aligned action. Apply this to life. It's not reserved for business. I started praying for the women I used to judge. I stopped associating with the women who gossiped all the time. I took responsibility for my behavior and, ultimately, the outcome I was craving. I stopped obsessing over what I could've done better and praised myself for giving my all, doing the best I could in situations, and staying the course when life got tough. I started appreciating myself and the people in my life who supported me, even though my success is not dependent upon having support. I started respecting women who spoke up for what they wanted and learned from them. Confidence is an energy, a vibe! It's contagious. Money is too!

Something magical happens when you start appreciating yourself for where you're at and who you are in the present moment. When I stopped apologizing for being different, I started to feel better. I started giving love more freely, first to myself, and then of course it became so much safer and easier for me to give love freely to others. It's not possible to love another person unconditionally if you cannot first give that same kind of love and acceptance to yourself. It's not possible to receive abundant opportunities if you are feeling miserable and stuck in a *why hasn't it happened for me yet* mindset.

Whenever you feel down, lost, or confused, it's almost second nature to get caught up in all the things that are wrong in your life. When you actively stop that thought pattern and create a new behavior of focusing on the truth—you are okay as you are, things will get better, and you will get through whatever it is that's got you down—you open the door to freedom from repeating the cycle of self-destruction, freedom from chaotic, racing thoughts, and, most importantly, freedom from expecting yourself to be anything less than who you are.

Oftentimes, we as women brainwash ourselves into thinking that if we don't do things right or we don't get the result we want right away (think fad diet gone bad or manifesting your first million overnight), we punish ourselves for not measuring up. We convince ourselves we could have done more and should have done better. Basically, we apologize for being human along with our perceived failures and run away from the lesson. The lesson is to trust yourself and to trust in God's ability and desire to give you what you want. Trust is a knowing; it does not waver.

When we stop apologizing, we no longer suffer in silence with imposter syndrome, and we start feeling lighter and more in control of ourselves. In turn, our self-esteem rises. I know it, and you know it. We are good enough as we are, and we cannot get to where we're going if we don't acknowledge that, honor ourselves in the process, and take the pressure off of ourselves. You'll never have what you want in life if you're apologizing for wanting it. You are blocking your blessings if you feel bad about wanting them.

Want your relationships to improve, to lose that extra ten pounds, or to learn a new skill? Cool! Be gentle with yourself in the process. Most of your perceived failures are impossible starts. Why impossible? Because you set yourself up to be let down. You expect yourself to be disappointed, frustrated, broke, overtired, hungry (or should I say hangry!) because that's how it's always been, and those expectations will come true unless you change the energy of the expectation. You think you should do it all right away, in the right way, and, therefore, well, you do not succeed. When you shift your mindset and focus on growing, evolving, and becoming the woman you desire to be, it leads to better outcomes, inner peace, and more certainty. Those things are the gateway to making more money.

You have the power within you to completely change your life. The better you feel, the easier it gets.

Stop apologizing for being you.

Start valuing yourself.

Release the urge to be someone else's idea of perfect and start being more of who you are. It's scary at times but oh so worth it. Get in touch with who you are, what you like, and what you don't like. Stop worrying about what people say about you and think about you. *Care more about what you think about you.* You must care more about how you feel than how other people feel about you.

PS. The best part of no longer apologizing to others is you get to accept where you are, forgive yourself for trying to be someone you're not, and start putting the pieces back together just the way you want them to be. As they say, you do you, boo! It's primetime to shine!

A Prayer for Guidance

Dear God, I have been afraid of going after my dreams because I worry about what people will think of me. Help me to release those fears. Help me to care more about what I think about me. I am ready to break the cycle of seeking approval. I am ready to receive guidance on my next step. I have big dreams and big desires, and I want to believe they are possible for me. I am looking for relief. I am willing to take action and to believe in myself. I am ready to receive in a next level way. Thank you. Amen.

CHAPTER 23

Confession: I Levelled Up My Lingerie

I had to throw away the tiny undies I was wearing that definitely didn't fit me properly anymore but continued to take up space in my drawer for far too long and buy several pairs of well-fitted panties that fit my booty! What's with women and underwear anyway? This is where you laugh and nod your head in acknowledgment of having kept your own not-so-flattering-don't-fit-right panties, right? You know you've got some old ratty pairs hidden in that drawer too. You keep them around because they are well worn and have served you well. Certain times of the month call for certain underwear. It's not about bikini or thong; it's about comfort. Guess what, ladies? It's time to clear the clutter, and that includes all the old socks and underwear you've got bunched up in your drawer. When you clear out the old, you make room for the new. Panties, lingerie, overstuffed closets, junk drawers—you name it, it matters! Clutter causes chaos.

If you are ready to step into the luxe lifestyle you desire to live, you've got to upgrade your environment, and that includes your wardrobe. You've heard the saying, pull up your big girl panties and deal with it? It's important that as you upgrade your thoughts, your habits, and your standards of living, you upgrade your panties. Deal with it, they say. I say *create it*—your dream life, that is. Fancy panties and all. It sounds simple and something that you don't need to be told how to do, but what I know for sure is a lot of women slack off in the lingerie department. They don't have any that fits, or they don't feel comfortable spending money on the good-quality stuff. C'mon, sis! You know that cheap lingerie falls apart after one wash. Why do I care? Because how you do one thing is how you do everything. Women who cheap out on their panties are cheaping out on their dreams too. The woman you want to be is waiting for you to welcome her in. She's knocking on your door, begging you to unleash her into this world. It's time to write your own set of rules and throw away the outdated contracts you made with all the wrong people. It's time to upgrade everything and that includes dressing like the woman you want to be. Nobody feels good when their panties are in a bunch. Facts!

Living life on your terms involves cutting ties with all that no longer belongs in your life, and that includes your lingerie drawer. You've conformed to the social norm for too long. You are bursting with excitement and ready to embrace your soul desires with confidence and ease.

Conformity is all about matching the beliefs, attitudes, and behaviors that are perceived as normal to a particular social group or society. Just because your friend shops at Walmart for everything doesn't mean you have to.

I stopped doing what society told me to do a long time ago. My hunger to live authentically overpowered my inner child's need for approval. You can't live your best life if you exert all your energy trying to fit in or be considered a good woman, a good wife, a good mom, and, most importantly, a good Christian. There's nothing worse than those people who hide behind a scripture in the Bible to judge others. You know what I'm talking about, don't you? You also know that people will judge you no matter what you do, so you might as well be doing life your way. You've stayed a prisoner to the fear of outgrowing your normal long enough. When women change their hair and their underwear style, everything else changes too! Don't believe me. Do it and see for yourself.

You see, as a woman who was raised on the principle that children were seen and not heard, I had conformed long enough. It's no wonder I shine brightest when writing or speaking to a crowd. I have a lot to say, and I'm not afraid to say it.

You might be sitting on the fence, one foot is dangling over and the other securely standing on the bottom rail. You are scared about what lies ahead for you if you take that next step. You're frozen. It's uncomfortable. You will never know how fabulous your life can be if you don't jump the fence. I know too many women on the edge of change who are hanging on to their old, familiar ways for dear life when what's waiting for them on the other side is magnificent and blissful. I can appreciate that it's not easy, but neither is living life from a state of mediocrity, sitting on a ripped couch covered with an old floral blanket from the eighties, in a pair of ripped panties, scraping the bottom of an ice-cream tub, wishing for better days.

When I found myself in a similar position, I started tapping into my core beliefs, personal values, and desires. I committed to creating my life the way I wanted it. First things first, I got clear on what that looked like for me. What does that look like for you?

I had to dive into wealth consciousness work. My money story was fifty shades of messed up. I upgraded my panties, and at the same time, I upgraded my relationship with money. Why buy the cheap Fruit of the Loom low-rise when the Victoria Secret thong fits and feels so much better? It wasn't just an emotional upgrade; it was a financial upgrade. Women will spend six dollars on a latte but won't dish out the dough for nice undergarments. We are a weird breed sometimes.

I allowed myself to spend money on myself completely guilt-free. I felt like a true rebel.

There's always that one person who takes a jab at you no matter how much you've accomplished, or how healthy your child's lunch is, or how organized your home is, or what idea you come up with in the boardroom, or what handbag you carry. You know what I mean, don't you? That one person who stirs things up in you that no one else can stir up. The one person you allow to get under your skin. When we stay stuck in that vibe, we go against our natural state and inner being—definitely not ideal if you want to build mental and emotional wellness in your world. You've got to find your own voice. You've got to break the habit of living to please and start living to impact. If you want a fancy life, start doing things and buying things that generate that feeling inside of you. There is nothing better than wearing well-fitted lace panties under your dress, rocking your pumps, hair brushed and curled, with some glitzy earrings to announce how badass and fierce you are when you enter the room. The panties part, well, nobody needs to know that, but what I'm getting at is the *feeling*. When you take care of yourself, you feel better, and how you dress says a lot about how you're feeling about yourself. Besides, I haven't met a woman that feels confident when her underwear is digging in and showing the world things they don't need to see.

It's time for you to start dressing the part of the woman you want to be. Think about it. Does the next-level you dress up, down, both? Does she wear lipstick or gloss? Is she into perfume or body spray? Get specific and follow suit. There is no room for second best at this point in your self-care journey. There's also no apologizing. Some of the most beautiful and successful women I know rock their yoga pants, bun, and dangling earrings with such a vibe it's incredible. Other beautiful and successful women I know love to get dressed up—heels, makeup, hair, nails, lashes, all of it. They're all amazing. There is no right or wrong way to own your fierce factor. You know what these beautiful and successful women do have in common? They splurge on their undergarments. Twisted knickers ruin your outfit, and they can ruin your confidence. Want to start upgrading your wardrobe? Start with your lingerie. Spend the money on better fabric and change your life!

I started visualizing myself asserting myself in conversations, at networking events, in business meetings, and in all the things marriage and parenting. When I would see myself as the woman who confidently asserted herself, she was dressed well, feeling on top of the world, and not apologizing for it.

Listen to me: there are people who are terrified of your success. They feel threatened by your determination to pursue your goals. The more confidence you exude, the more fear they feel. This includes being able to shop at higher quality stores. Do it anyway.

People will be upset. Those people are your family, your friends, and strangers on the internet who are not taking responsibility for their own lives. There is a difference between confidence and arrogance, and women have been reluctant to express their desires or belief in themselves to attain them because of the fear of being judged. Not anymore! Not a woman like you. You deserve to feel amazing and live an incredible life. That involves dressing well, upgrading your wardrobe, and not putting yourself last on the list. Throw out those old saggy bras that don't hold you up and treat yourself to ones that do.

Wear success your way. That's the same message I shared in my book *PRIMETIME Success*. It's imperative for your well-being to stay true to who you are and your personal values, no matter how much awesomeness you attract and experience. Every up level will require more of you. It gets to be fun, and it gets to feel good.

Inevitably, Ms. Fierce, you'll have to upgrade your panties! Yes, that means actually upgrading to big-girl panties, as in becoming the adult in your life. Get back into the driver's seat and hit the gas, baby! You've got places to go, and there are so many people rooting for you. Those people are your supportive family members, your new friends who you've met along your journey, and yes, even the girl working at your favorite lingerie boutique.

See the irony there?

Becoming the adult in your life is critical on your self-care journey. Adulting requires taking responsibility for your life—the good, bad, the ugly, and the great. It means no longer pointing your finger and looking within at all the things; we have the power to change. It includes changing how you think and function. Working as a mental health counselor and success coach for many years has allowed me to learn about and appreciate the significance of caring for your inner child. *However*, you aren't ten anymore, and it's up to you to adult in a way that allows you to, yes, care for your inner child but also to live as an adult. As I said in *PRIMETIME Success*, you don't need a participation ribbon in order to feel good enough.

Girl, it's time to level up your lingerie.

A Prayer for Guidance

Dear God, I've been reluctant to spend money on myself. I am starting to make money doing what I love, yet I still feel guilty when I buy myself things. Help me to see the connection between taking care of myself and my ability to attract more money. I like feeling good, and I like to buy quality clothes. It sounds trite, but I need help giving myself permission to upgrade my wardrobe alongside my lifestyle. I am so grateful for my blessings. Thank you. Amen.

CHAPTER 24

Confession: I Am Your Royal Highness

Growing up, I was addressed by two primary names, Your Royal Highness by my mother and Young Lady by my dad—each of which was reserved for times when my attitude was showing. My inner elitist princess called for *Your Royal Highness,* and my stubborn side required *Young Lady* ("you'll do as your told" would follow those words).

In November 2014, I was struggling in ways nobody knew. I was bouncing between the palliative room my dad was slowly dying in to speaking on stages about empowerment and confidence building. During that month, I clocked thousands of miles on my car as I spent time with my mother and dad at the hospital and headed back home, a few hours away, to prepare my keynotes and tend to my pets. My bunny and fish were low maintenance but in need of attention nonetheless. That month will always be a blur. Emotionally, I tapped out and operated on autopilot because I had a job to do, and the man who raised me would want me to do it and do it well. I didn't tell any of the event organizers that my dad was in palliative care, dying, because they would have messed up my focus. To be honest, I didn't tell anybody.

I delivered exceptional keynotes and was well compensated. It was business as usual. Financially, I was doing okay. I had created my own business to fulfill my dreams and to have the impact I so desired to have. My business model allowed me to serve others in a way I wanted to and met my needs and lifestyle desires. It was a wonderful setup, albeit a work in progress. Hindsight is always twenty-twenty, right? Good thing I had established my own company because otherwise the weeks leading up to my dad's passing would have been so different.

I had worked for government-funded organizations for years, and not only was the pay less than desirable, but requesting time off from an already short-staffed agency was like pulling a boar's tooth. The final breath my dad took was both beautiful and devastating. I remember standing there, having just kissed his forehead, holding his hand, and feeling the life finally leave his deteriorating body. I don't remember what I said, but I do remember vowing to never take another breath for granted, ever again. I walked out of his hospital room and allowed myself to attempt to collect my thoughts. In that moment, the only thing that was clear was that my life would never be the same. I thought immediately about how I was going to emotionally support my son, the only grandchild at the time. Money can't soothe grief. Then my thoughts raced to my mother and to my husband. And of course, my clients. I made a decision to not only tend to all of my responsibilities, I committed to having everything I have ever wanted and so much more. Life is precious. Time is money.

The next few weeks were a blur. My son had to return to school; we had pulled him out because, well, family trumps textbooks. I got back to business as usual, only nothing was usual. Everything was different. I sat in my morning journal sessions and completely re-evaluated my life, my relationships, and my business. If I was going to honor my commitment to never take a breath for granted, I would have some work to do to live the life I desired. I was only living at half of my potential. I was still playing small. I was still pretending to be okay with parts of my life that were slowly eating away at me, and I wasn't going to pretend anything anymore. I realized I simply couldn't afford to. My elite inner princess was demanding more.

I did something drastic. It was one of the hardest decisions I had to make. I decided I was no longer going to be available for *fine*. I was no longer going to settle for less of anything that I desired—love, travel, money, and liberated freedom to fully accept myself and live bolder. I took a blind leap of faith in me, myself, and I. This whole book has shared different self-care practices I have implemented along my journey to living my best life. Years ago, that saying was foreign to me. I thought my life was good as it was and that it was selfish to want more than what I already had.

Diving into personal development has taught me that our entire purpose here on earth is to grow, evolve, and expand. Watching my dad leave the physical world shook me to my core and woke me up all in the same breath. We are here for a reason, and we have so many possibilities at our fingertips. If we choose to acknowledge that and take action, we can create whatever life we desire. Remember in chapter one, when I explored identity? I officially acknowledged and accepted my role as the co-creator in my life. I got clear on who I wanted to be and committed to receiving all that I was asking for. I got intentional about everything—my health, my marriage, my parental responsibilities, my business, and my friendships. I started to trust that things were happening *for* me and not *to* me. I refused to play victim, and I refused to hold space for anyone else in my life who tried to. You cannot live an amazing, vibrant life if you blame everyone for everything that has happened to you. That's such a low-vibe kind of lifestyle. There comes a point you own your role in relationships and situations, choose to forgive and release, and move on with your life. People who choose not to do that will suck the life right out of you.

Taking ownership of my thoughts, my actions, and my energy changed everything. When you learn to fully believe in yourself and trust yourself, you generate high vibes everywhere you go. Your energy speaks before you walk into a room, and it's no different when you're home alone. The universe is responding to your vibration all the time. I'd never asked with true clarity for what I wanted before, nor did I have the energy of receiving precisely that which I desired behind my ask. As a result of that, oftentimes I didn't get what I so deeply desired and instead got something either similar to or completely opposite of it. I share this because *a clear ask* is vital to receiving what you desire to receive or something better.

Self-care includes believing in yourself and your abilities to have all the things you want. I mean, ladies, it's one thing to be bold and ask for what your heart desires, and it is a totally other thing to actually expect to receive it without micromanaging the how and when and allowing greatness to happen. Honoring my elitist inner princess allowed me to expect that everything I wanted would be mine. That's where faith comes in. Work that spiritual muscle, girl.

I have since graduated to queen energy, but I love that my husband still calls me his princess.

You have to know at your core how valuable and worthy you are simply because you exist, not for any reason other than that. Honestly. You would not be here reading my book if your purpose on earth was done. When you ask for something, you must believe you are worthy to receive it and take the necessary action toward having it. Behaving as Your Royal Highness may not have served me well as a child, but the name stuck, and I have since owned my place in my own royal family. The funny truth is, since my son was born, I have always called him Prince. I always will. He is royalty to me. Of course, as his mother, I feel strongly that he is the most incredible man in the world. So be it. I'm sure you feel the same about your child. Children are our greatest teachers. I can't stop because he is watching me. He watches how I deal with change, loss, and money!

Think about how much energy you spend worrying about money, relationships, and future events. Channel that energy into the here and now and start owning your role in your family, in your career, in your life. It's such a liberating and empowering feeling to unabashedly own your space in this world. To stand up and say, "I matter!"

In the coaching work I am privileged to facilitate with women all around the world, it is clear that they share the common belief pattern that making money doing what you love is possible—but how? How good can it really get? Stepping up and being visible in our world used to be considered unsafe for women. We are supposed to swallow our feelings and tolerate what we receive in life, so as to fulfill the expected pattern of generations of women before us. The divide between women has become more about *who does she think she is* more so than *she leads, and by leading, I am empowered to lead myself.* See the difference in mindset?

Not anymore! Times have changed. Women are becoming incredibly successful in the business world and doing such great work while being well compensated. It's exciting! The more women declare their worth and own their abilities to make their dreams come true, the more love and light that is spread afar. When one woman rises up and says, "I am here, and I will not apologize for being here," the more women feel a sense of self-permission to do the same. Ask for what you want, sis, and expect to receive it. Open your mind and your arms and embrace the possibilities. Life gets to be fun. It gets to be way less complicated than what you're making it. Unleash your desires. Write them down, speak them out loud, and trust they have been placed in your heart for a reason. God does not mess around.

How will you ever receive your heart's desires if you think it's always so hard? And how can you receive your abundant blessings if you're closed off to what's possible for you?

You can't, sis!

Money. Financial health. Wealth. Abundance. Financial freedom.

It's always about your energy and what you believe to be true for you.

Keep that in mind as you read this chapter.

Have you ever had a dream? Something that you wanted so badly but never knew how you'd get it, or maybe you wondered if it was even possible for you?

I grew up in a small village, population of a few hundred, which included the homes along the country roads. So, my dreams were usually squashed quickly by everybody who was family or friends. Unintentionally, I'm sure, but squashed nonetheless. Girls from my hometown had an unspoken job to grow up to be wives, moms, and church clerks. An expectation of being a *good* girl. Cool, if that's what you want to do with your life. It's not so cool if you have huge, audacious dreams like me *and* you believe they are possible—or if you are a woman who doesn't want to drive a minivan around, full of kids arguing, while you pretend to be oh so fulfilled! If that fulfills you, awesome! If it doesn't, don't apologize about it.

When I stopped accepting other people's expectations for my life as what I had to do, everything changed for me. Sounds cheesy, I know. Everybody and their sister are saying it nowadays, but for me, and perhaps for you, it's true. I don't really remember when I decided to stop settling. I didn't use that language at that time in my journey. I just remember feeling exhausted and at times resentful that I was always helping others, yet not once having anyone return the help. I remember wondering why I didn't feel good when helping others was the career path, I had chosen many years ago. My entire existence had become all about helping others, but at what cost? Losing my dad made it clear that time is not to be wasted.

I was sacrificing my dreams to be of free service to others. I didn't have a big meltdown or anything like that, but I did catch myself journaling one morning about wanting more freedom and to feel less responsibility for other people and their problems. I was writing down all of my huge aspirations and focused on the power in creating my reality to fit the vision in my head, yet here I was spending more time and energy helping others create their desired reality than my own. Messed up, eh?

Helping others who appreciate it and respect your time and energy is a different feeling than people expecting your help whenever they need it but aren't available to help you. So that was a pivotal moment in time when I said, "No more settling." I'm not 100 percent sure when it happened; it just did. It may have been when I moved out west at eighteen, or it may not have been until I decided to leave my first husband. Either way, it was pivotal. I was totally embarrassing my family, I'm sure, but at that point, I'd figured out that my happiness mattered more to me than anyone else's. I had spent the first twenty-three years of my life trying to please other people, and all it did was make me feel like crap inside. It was not an easy pursuit of carefree living. I will tell you that much. Both of those moments in time were very significant in my growth as a woman. Trust is built when you follow your heart and listen to your soul.

I had to figure out what I wanted and what I needed to function above mediocre. I had to own my role in the relationships and circumstances too. Little Miss Perfect isn't so perfect!

I had gone from struggling with low self-esteem, insecure as all get out, full of fear and near poverty, to putting myself through college while raising my baby as a single mama, working three jobs, and trying to be a good Christian woman.

At that time, I felt broken. In retrospect, I was not broken. I was putting my life together, and I was more courageous than I had ever been.

It's funny how we criticize ourselves for the same things we praise others for going through and keeping their head in the game. Can you relate to that? Do you ever catch yourself beating yourself up for something that actually deserves recognition for sticking it out and persevering through it? I have. I had to learn how to transform that kind of critical self-talk into positive self-talk. I had to stop expecting perfection and accept that I was a work in progress. Aren't we all, really? You know what else? I had to ask for help.

More importantly, I had to learn how to *accept* help.

Oh, my word! That was so difficult for me for many reasons. It was also a life lesson: asking for what you need is part of adulting.

I transferred that skill into my relationships and in my business. I have an incredible marriage and family because of it. My husband and I host The PRIMETIME HUMP Day Show each Wednesday on my Facebook page. We truly desire to teach other couples that they, too, can have it all. When you love yourself and confidently ask for what you need, every relationship you have improves. Success to me is having great health and an incredible marriage and family bond, and serving others while making exceptional money.

If you've ever had to ask for money, you will understand the embarrassment and humility in doing so. Same goes for asking for help with childcare, or transportation, or whatever it might be. I mean, if any of you have ever been mom-shamed, you get that it's almost taboo for a woman, let alone a mother, to ask for or need help.

Aren't we supposed to show up as Wonder Woman for all to see? Where's your cape? Mine is in the trash, along with others' expectations of how I should be living.

PSA: No woman can do it all on her own all the time, and neither can any man.

Here's the thing though. If we don't ask for what we want and need, then we have zero reasons to feel frustrated that we don't have those things in our lives. We must stop asking for permission to be who we want to be and just go for it. All in. No more dipping your toes! Your Royal Highness at your service. How may I support you in creating your best life?

Self-care is not for the faint at heart, and it's not about filtering out the not-so-great moments either. That's the thing about life. We all need help sometimes, and there is nothing abnormal about that, ever. Practice asking for what you need and want, and build that confidence muscle.

Why women pretend to be doing it all, I do not know, and I don't have the time to try to figure it out. With that being said, I quickly shifted my perspective to view asking for what I needed as an act of courage and assertiveness.

Here's the other thing I did. This is a biggie. I *expected* to receive what I asked for. Faith at its finest. I totally expect everything I ask for to show up for me when I need it. If what I ask for does not show up for me, that means something even better is on its way to me.

Take a moment and ask yourself these two questions:

1. Who do I need to become to have all the things I desire?
2. What thoughts need to evolve in order to receive the abundance I ask for?

It's one thing to ask for what you want; it's another thing to be completely certain you will receive it. To stand in certainty that you get to have it all and it gets to be easy. Let's explore an abundance mindset for a minute here. The word *abundance* means to have a lot of something. If you work on building your self-esteem, focus on positive self-talk, and start identifying what you need, the next step is asking for it and trusting you will receive it.

You deserve great things, and you will attract great things and people into your life based on your energy, attitude, and belief in yourself. If all you do is think negative thoughts about your current situation or relationship, then you can expect a lot more negativity to surround you. It's the law of attraction at work here. Google Abraham Hicks if you have zero idea of what I'm talking about. You are not here to live in your past or in people-pleasing mode. Shocking, I know, but it's true. You are here to grow, shift, and mature throughout your life journey, and that includes learning how to ask for what you need and being open to receive it. I have repeated that message in every chapter for a reason.

What would it feel like to live life on your terms, confidently moving through situations and experiences with no guilt about having what you want, money included?

A Prayer for Guidance

Dear God, I have come a long way on my journey. I am starting to feel more and more confident in who I am. I trust that you want me to live a great life full of health and abundance. Help me to assert myself more, knowing it is safe for me to receive everything my heart desires, big or small. Thank you for the endless blessings in my life. I am ready to receive more. Amen.

POWER THOUGHTS FOR FINANCIAL FREEDOM

I am worthy of financial freedom.

Money loves me.

I am worthy of receiving my desires and more.

I trust myself with money.

I am a money magnet.

I am wealthy beyond my wildest dreams.

I am grateful for the flow of money in my life.

I choose to create a rich and fulfilling life.

I have the power to create the success and wealth I desire.

I am free of debt and live in abundance.

I am financially blessed.

I am a vibrational match for the money I desire.

Money serves a purpose in my life.

I am so divinely taken care of.

Wealth and abundance are my birthright.

I open my arms to receive all the money I desire and more.

Lightning Source UK Ltd.
Milton Keynes UK
UKHW012133120121
376933UK00006B/369/J